Project Management

Donna Deeprose

T0341793

- *The* fast track route to mastering all aspects of project management

- Covers the key areas of project management, from tools to teams, and from planning and executing an individual project to managing an enterprise by projects

- Examples, cases and ideas from some of the world's top companies, including Nortel Networks, Gartner, Siemens and Chiyoda Corporation

- Includes a glossary of key concepts and a comprehensive resources guide

OPERATIONS

06.06

≫EXPRESS EXEC.COM≪
essential management thinking at your fingertips

Copyright © Capstone Publishing 2002

The right of Donna Deeprose to be identified as the author of this work has been asserted in accordance with the Copyright, Designs and Patents Act 1988

First published 2002 by
Capstone Publishing (A Wiley Company)
8 Newtec Place
Magdalen Road
Oxford OX4 1RE
United Kingdom
http://www.capstoneideas.com

CIP catalogue records for this book are available from the British Library and the US Library of Congress

ISBN 1-84112-222-X

FSC

Mixed Sources
Product group from well-managed
forests and other controlled sources

Cert no. SGS-COC-2953
www.fsc.org
© 1996 Forest Stewardship Council

Substantial discounts on bulk quantities of Capstone books are available to corporations, professional associations and other organizations. Please contact Capstone for more details on +44 (0)1865 798 623 or (fax) +44 (0)1865 240 941 or (e-mail) info@wiley-capstone.co.uk

Contents

Introduction to ExpressExec   v

06.06.01 Introduction   1
06.06.02 Definition of Terms   5
06.06.03 Evolution   11
06.06.04 The E-Dimension   21
06.06.05 The Global Dimension   29
06.06.06 The State of the Art   41
06.06.07 In Practice   57
06.06.08 Key Concepts and Thinkers   77
06.06.09 Resources   89
06.06.10 Ten Steps to Making it Work   99

Frequently Asked Questions (FAQs)   113
Index   115

Introduction to ExpressExec

ExpressExec is 3 million words of the latest management thinking compiled into 10 modules. Each module contains 10 individual titles forming a comprehensive resource of current business practice written by leading practitioners in their field. From brand management to balanced scorecard, ExpressExec enables you to grasp the key concepts behind each subject and implement the theory immediately. Each of the 100 titles is available in print and electronic formats.

Through the ExpressExec.com Website you will discover that you can access the complete resource in a number of ways:

» printed books or e-books;
» e-content – PDF or XML (for licensed syndication) adding value to an intranet or Internet site;
» a corporate e-learning/knowledge management solution providing a cost-effective platform for developing skills and sharing knowledge within an organization;
» bespoke delivery – tailored solutions to solve your need.

Why not visit www.expressexec.com and register for free key management briefings, a monthly newsletter and interactive skills checklists. Share your ideas about ExpressExec and your thoughts about business today.

Please contact elound@wiley-capstone.co.uk for more information.

Introduction

» Why project teams are cropping up all over, even in functionally-organized companies
» The spread of the project management model from engineering to white collar industries
» The importance of project management skills to operations managers and individual contributors

Repeat after me – no, better yet, say these along with me; you know them all already.

» Do more with less.
» Faster, better, cheaper.
» The only constant is change.
» Push accountability down.
» Empower workers.

There they are – the business mantras of the past couple of decades. Most of them were born during the high-flying 1980s, but they took on new urgency with the economic downturn of the early 1990s. Dedication to these maxims became even more passionate as the economy, fueled by accelerated change and new technologies, exploded into one of the longest running growth periods in modern times. Then, lest anyone become complacent, the massive layoffs that accompanied the slowdown of 2000–2001 again reminded everyone that this was no time to relax and rest on last year's laurels.

The thing is, the mantras aren't just clichés. Companies that succeed in empowering workers and pushing accountability down are able to do more with less, and do it faster and better. They are flexible enough not only to swing with the changes the outside world imposes, but also to swiftly generate their own changes, creating and maximizing new opportunities.

MANAGING BY PROJECTS

More and more, companies are achieving these advantages by assigning the pursuit of opportunities and the solution of problems not to operations units but to project teams – temporary, cross-functional groups each with a unique purpose, a defined budget, and a scheduled timeframe. It's the team's job to determine how it will meet its purpose, carry out its tasks, complete its goals – and then disband.

Never anticipating permanence, project teams are ideally adapted to constantly changing needs, prospects, and environments. Charged with fulfilling a defined purpose, project team members are accountable for achieving it and empowered to determine and implement the best way of doing so.

It's not a new model, of course. Engineering and construction firms have been doing it for years. That's how buildings and bridges, and even spaceships, got built. But in white-collar industries and manufacturing, where the traditional model of layered management, functional serfdoms, and ongoing repetitive work still held sway, the movement toward managing by projects has been nothing short of a revolution. And it is gathering momentum.

As they join the revolution, companies find it's not enough to pull together a team of people with the composite skills and tell them, "Go ahead." As the engineers have known all along, project teams need a set of tools and methodologies that have been tested and proven to guide and support a project from conception to successful completion. These are the instruments of project management that white collar and manufacturing companies are borrowing from engineering and applying to their own projects.

So the US group of a global insurance company has an office of project management to support the hundreds of projects going on at any given time throughout the company. In the manufacturing division of a giant cosmetics company, almost 100% of the division's capital budget is managed through projects, supported through an office of capital budgeting and project management. An international pharmaceutical firm provides project support through professional project managers in the office of change management. These companies aren't unusual; they are examples of a growing trend.

For individuals, this trend presents a new career prospect that promises to be one of the most exciting opportunities in business in the next decade – the professional project manager. There will be an increasing demand for people who can manage the process of planning, implementing, controlling, and successfully closing down major projects – while motivating a team of disparate individuals to work in concert toward a shared goal.

But all the work won't be assigned to professional project managers. To an ever-greater degree, operations managers and individual contributors are being called upon to take on project work in addition to their ongoing tasks. Management guru Tom Peters anticipates a time when all white-collar work will be project work. Traditional ways of working are too slow, he maintains, and too hard to place a value on.

But until that day happens, you can expect to split your time among your ongoing operations work, a team or two that you'll lead, and a few more that you'll contribute your expertise to as a member.

Without a managing-by-projects mentality, your organization won't be able to keep up in a constantly changing environment. Without project management skills, you won't be able to stay on top of the challenges you'll face.

But one thing is sure – with the skills to work this way, you'll never be bored!

Definition of Terms

» What distinguishes projects from ongoing work
» Three big differences between project management and operations management
» Characteristics of a project team
» What makes a project successful

The best way to begin a discussion of any topic is with a definition of terms. Dedicating this chapter to that purpose creates a clear context and minimizes misunderstandings in the chapters that follow, which really delve into the subject.

Let's get clear on the key terms.

WHAT IS A PROJECT?

The word *project* seems simple enough, but, in fact, we toss it around to cover a wide range of activities. "My Saturday project is to clean my closet," someone might say. Or, at the other extreme, "Building a pyramid was quite a project." And, indeed, if you stretch the definition of project far enough, both closet and pyramid qualify, but they both fall outside the parameters of the word as we'll use it here.

The kind of project for which you're going to have to hone your project management skills can be described as:

"The work that needs to be done to produce a unique, predefined outcome within a predetermined period of time and budget."

(By that definition, we can drop the closet cleaning because there is no budget involved, and the pyramid building because we have no idea whether or not there was a predetermined period of time for completion. Or to put it on more obvious grounds, the closet project is too small and the pyramid too big to fit in this book.)

Two key parts of the project definition distinguish it from the ongoing work of any organization.

The first is the word "unique." The goal of every project is a one-of-a-kind outcome. That doesn't have to mean that nothing remotely like it has ever been done before. But nothing exactly like it has. Your company may put together a project team to produce an annual report every year. But every year that report is different from every other year's. So the team can, and should, take advantage of the previous year's experiences, but it can't simply copy the old report.

The second key feature is the predetermined timeframe. Of course, there is nothing so flexible as a deadline, but its existence signals that there will be an end to this activity. The bible of project management,

The Guide to the Project Management Body of Knowledge – more commonly known as the *PMBOK® Guide* (pronounced "pimbok" and published by the Project Management Institute) – emphasizes the temporary nature of a project: It has a definite beginning and a definite end.

That doesn't mean that once complete, the project output never needs more work. If you build a Website or a skyscraper, somebody is going to have to maintain it. If you create a training program, somebody's going to have to run it over and over and keep records on who's attended. If you design an electronic hula hoop, somebody's going to have to produce it in great numbers, day in and day out. But the maintenance, the repeated facilitation, the administration, and the production aren't project work. They are ongoing work and they fall into the operations side of the business.

Here's another way to look at the project/ongoing work contrast: A wedding is a project; staying married is ongoing work.

PROJECT MANAGEMENT: WHAT MAKES IT DIFFERENT?

Project management is the discipline of guiding a project from conception to completion. It requires the application of appropriate skills, techniques, and tools so that the project is completed to specifications, on time, and within budget.

When you contrast it with operations management, three big differences spring to mind:

1 *Its tools.* Thanks to the engineers who started it all, project management has a set of tested tools and validated processes that make operations management look like flying by the seat of your pants. To the uninitiated, these tools and processes are a little intimidating, with names like PERT Chart, critical path, Gantt Chart, responsibility assignment matrix, added value analysis, and in recent years, software programs like Microsoft Project®.

Novices often begin by viewing the manual tools as a pain in the neck. Depending upon their inclination, they expect the software to be utterly beyond comprehension or the answer to all their prayers. In fact, project management tools won't do your work for you but they will help you map a route to your goal and make course corrections with the least amount of pain when changing conditions or unexpected situations occur.

Depending upon the magnitude of your project, you may not need them all, but tackling a project without any of them is a little like building a house without hammer or nails.

2 *Its heavy emphasis on planning.* Pick up any popular book on project management and you'll find that it gets to actually doing the work about half way through. Up to that point it's all about planning. And even then, a big part of managing the execution of the project is reworking the plan to keep progress on tasks in sync with the plan and the plan in sync with progress.

In operations management, there's nothing that quite matches this single-minded focus on planning the work and working the plan. If you manage an operating unit, you probably write an annual business plan, laying out *what* you expect to accomplish in the upcoming year. You don't need to get deeply into *how* you will do that, first, because upper management doesn't want that much detail, and second, because for the most part you're going to continue doing what you did before.

But the value of a project plan is in its specificity and details. That's how projects succeed.

3 *The special relationship between manager and team.* The traditional definition of management is getting work done through other people. Project managers do that, just as operations managers do. The difference is that project managers usually have to get their work done through people who don't report to them.

Except for the largest projects, most project teams are made up of people from various parts of the organization lent to the project part-time. Their first commitment is to their ongoing job. Their first loyalty is to their work unit manager. They'll devote themselves wholeheartedly to a project not out of duty, but only out of passion. It's the project manager's job to instill that passion for the project not only in the team members but also, to a degree, in the members' work unit managers, who must sign off on the team members' participation in the first place and whose willingness to lend their employees must be continually renewed.

The relationship between manager and team is where the reality of project management diverges from the image of single-minded fixation on charts and tables and schedules. In fact, among leading practitioners and writers, who come out of the engineering world, there's a growing suspicion that planning and scheduling aren't the most important parts of the project manager's job. Dr Harold Kerzner, professor of systems management at Baldwin-Wallace College, has spent 35 years practicing, studying, and teaching project management and has authored nearly 20 books on the subject. After all that, he says, "I have come to the belief that project management is more than planning and scheduling, but also working with teams, motivating them, getting them to complete the objective. The behavioral side is more important than quantitative techniques."

THE PROJECT TEAM: CRITICAL CHARACTERISTICS

In their influential book, *The Wisdom of Teams*, John R. Katzenbach and Douglas K. Smith gave us the seminal definition of team:

"A team is a small number of people with complementary skills who are committed to a common purpose, performance goals, and approach for which they hold themselves mutually accountable"[1]

While organizations toss the word team at everything from a small, self-managed work unit to a division of thousands, nowhere does Katzenbach and Smith's definition fit better than in a project team where:

» *members have a common purpose and they need each other to attain it*. In an operations unit, employees often have nearly identical skills, and they work independently alongside each other. A project needs a team of people with a variety of skills who coordinate their work to achieve a joint result;
» *team members agree on goals to achieve the purpose, tasks to meet the goals, and standards for success*. It's important to remember that these are team responsibilities, not one-person tasks for the project manager;

» *members hold themselves individually and collectively account-able for team results.* This doesn't happen automatically just because people are assigned to the project. But you know a group has matured into a real team when members react to a problem not by pointing fingers and placing blame but by joint problem solving to be sure it doesn't happen again.

FINALLY, HOW DO YOU DEFINE SUCCESS?

The classic definition of project success is:

"Meeting specifications, on time, and within budget."

By a strict interpretation of that definition, some studies have shown that at least 80% of all projects fail. So a realistic definition has to accommodate deadline and budget revisions and even changed goals.

But even a more accommodating definition leaves out what may be the most important criterion:

"Satisfying the customer."

You can substitute the word stakeholder for customer if you like, or define customer very broadly: anyone who is going to be affected by your project. The list certainly begins with a paying customer if you have one, but it also includes anyone in your organization who is going to use the product or service you produce, as well as anyone in management who has staked even a particle of his or her reputation on your project's outcome.

A project is a success when the project team, management, and customers are all satisfied that the outcome meets specifications in terms of goals, time, and budget.

NOTE

1 Katzenbach, J. R. & Smith, D. K. (1993) *The Wisdom of Teams.* HarperBusiness, New York.

Evolution

» The origin of the first modern project management tool
» Project management in the defense industry during and following WWII
» How project management matured in the space program
» The growth of associations that professionalized project management
» The emergence in the '90s of project-based organizations

The historians agree that modern project management was born in the military in the late stages of World War II, grew into young adulthood with the space program of the 1960s, branched out from its engineering home into the broader world of business in the 1980s, and grew into a prominent movement across industry lines in the last decade of the twentieth century. Of course, its origins go back much further...

PRE-HISTORY

They may not have had modern project management tools, but those pyramid builders surely knew something about getting projects done. Recent archeological discoveries suggest they didn't do it all by brute force. The unearthing of an architect's drawings for a very early pyramid shows that planning went into the task. And cemetery discoveries suggest that skilled tradespeople, not just slaves, contributed to the effort. That sounds like a cross-functional effort toward a unique, predetermined goal. These days we call that a project.

So be it a pyramid, a coliseum, a cathedral, or a nineteenth century railroad across the United States, the evidence of spectacular projects emphatically punctuates the story of human development.

PRECURSORS

Scientific management and the Gantt Chart

Early in the twentieth century, all the buzz in management circles was about Frederick Taylor's scientific management. Taylor advocated breaking work down into its most elementary components, performing time and motion studies to determine the fastest and most efficient way of performing every discrete task, and coaxing workers to perform that way by paying them significant bonuses. Taylor's theories influenced manufacturing and even white collar industries for much of the twentieth century, but in many respects, they were a far cry from project management, which takes a holistic view, focusing on outcomes.

While Taylor did his research in steel mills, his associate Henry Gantt was studying the management of Navy ship construction. Taylor's sights were on repetitive, ongoing work, whose outcomes changed little except in quantity, but Gantt's subjects did work that had a beginning and an end, culminating in the completion of a new ship. In other words, Gantt studied people who did project work.

Out of his research Gantt developed one of the most enduring of all scheduling tools, the Gantt Chart. A Gantt Chart is simply a bar chart with activities listed down the left side and dates along the top. Date-placed horizontal bars show the sequence of each activity and their scheduled and actual time. The Hoover Dam builders used Gantt Charts in the 1930s and they are still a favorite way to illustrate and track the sequencing of project tasks. You can draw one on a big wall calendar or, these days, you can call upon project management software to do it for you. The one drawn by your software won't be too different from the one Gantt introduced to the world in 1917, except perhaps for the embellishment of linking lines to show task dependencies.

Project management experts will stress that scheduling does not equate to project management, and they are right. Project management is much more. Nevertheless, scheduling is part of it, and the Gantt Chart was the first of the modern project management tools.

World War II and the Manhattan Project

In 1942, the US Government launched the Manhattan Project, a top-secret initiative whose goal was to develop a nuclear bomb before Germany did. In the three years before the first bomb was tested and continuing into 1946 when the project was closed down, its purpose broadened, first to force the surrender of Japan and second, to ensure post-war weapons ascendancy over the Soviet Union. Under the overall leadership of General Leslie R. Groves and the scientific direction of physicist J. Robert Oppenheimer, the project brought together a team of military, industrial, and scientific resources. As the layers of secrecy peeled away after the war, the planning, scheduling, and tracking techniques used to keep the project on target and the relationships among team members became an early model for the management of large military, engineering, and construction projects.

War's end and rebuilding

Meanwhile, across the Atlantic, peace arrived in Europe in 1944 and with it the need for vast public works projects to rebuild areas devastated by war. They didn't yet call it project management, but the

Institute of Civil Engineers of Great Britain spelled out some of the most important concepts in a report on post-war national development, which stated that "In order to carry out work efficiently, it is essential that a scheme of operations be first decided by those directly responsible for the execution. . . . With such planning the work can be broken down into a series of operations and an orderly sequence of execution evolved. . . . [This] does not mean, of course, that it is drawn up once and for all and cannot be changed. The exact opposite is true."[1]

MODERN PROJECT MANAGEMENT EVOLVES

The phrase "project management" made its way into the engineering vernacular in the 1950s, inspired largely by new methodologies being developed both in the military and in private industry.

Polaris and PERT

Back in the United States, the military of the 1950s embarked on weapons programs of such enormous complexity – both technically and organizationally – that managing them required new methods of planning, integrating, and controlling a vast array of tasks. Determination to build the Polaris missile in the shortest time possible spawned the development in 1958 of the Program Evaluation and Review Technique (PERT), a method for estimating the time required for each task and sequencing all tasks into one linked diagram leading logically to project completion. While PERT's specific method of combining worst case, best case, and most likely scenarios into one best time estimate isn't always followed anymore, it is the inspiration for all the network diagrams used for sequencing project tasks by today's project managers.

CPM and the private sector

While the US Navy's Polaris missile program proceeded down a PERT path, the private sector was creating project coordination tools of its own. Du Pont and Remington Rand Univac developed the Critical Path Method (CPM) in the late 1950s to coordinate plant maintenance projects. CPM is a method for identifying the shortest time to project completion by tracing the longest path through a network diagram. Far from competing with each other, PERT and CPM are so complementary that in popular project management terminology the two are often linked by a slash mark into PERT/CPM.

An out-of-this-world project

As an engineering prerogative, project management reached an apogee with the Apollo space program in the 1960s and 1970s. With Apollo, project management methodologies and tools emerged from the secret world of weapons development into the fishbowl of the space program, where the world watched every development. The statement of work – a detailed description of the tasks to be done – included in its contracts with outside providers and its status review and change control processes became models for project management everywhere.

The National Aeronautics and Space Administration (NASA) ran the program through a matrix organization where line operations, such as engineering and science, and staff functions like contracts, personnel, quality assurance, and legal provided resources and services to the project offices responsible for developing each program component. In the 1980s, private industry began to claim the matrix organization as its own, accompanied by all the hype that by this time heralded each new management fad. By the late 1990s, it was the underpinning for a new organization-wide approach to project management called enterprise project management or managing by projects – but that's getting ahead of our history.

GETTING ORGANIZED

In the 1960s, project managers around the world began to seek out each other to share best practices, coordinate research, and foster professionalism in project management. One of the first of these groups started in 1965 as a discussion group of managers of international projects. Calling itself INTERNET (which, for obvious reasons, it changed in 1994), the group held its first international Congress in 1967 in Vienna with participants from 30 different countries. Now known as the International Project Management Association (IPMA), the group has developed into an international network of about 30 national project management societies with a total membership of 20,000. Headquartered in Switzerland, its activities include conferences, seminars, training programs, certification, newsletters and journals, and research.

Just a few years after IPMA first began, a trio of Americans – one computer sales engineer and two of his clients – sat out a snowstorm that grounded the engineer's flight out of Philadelphia and tossed around ideas for improving project management tools and training people to use them. Out of their conversation, the idea of forming a national organization dedicated to managing projects took hold. In February 1968, the fledgling group held its first meeting and outlined its objectives.

1 Foster a recognition of the need for professionalism in project management.
2 Provide a forum for the free exchange of project management problems, solutions, and applications.
3 Coordinate industrial and educational research efforts with the objective of directing research efforts towards industrial problem areas.
4 Develop and disseminate common terminology and techniques in an effort to improve communications between users of project management systems.
5 Provide an interface between users and suppliers of both hardware and software systems.
6 Provide guidelines for instruction and education leading to project management implementation and encourage the career opportunities in the field of project management.[2]

In 1969, the group that began with a delayed flight became the Project Management Institute (PMI), founded "on the premise that there were many management practices that were common to projects in application areas as diverse as construction and pharmaceuticals."[3] The fledgling association was destined to grow into the world's largest project management organization with chapters worldwide and a current membership of more than 75,000.

PMI began accrediting project management programs provided by educational institutions in 1983 and certifying qualified Project Management Professionals (PMP®) in 1984. To become a PMP®, a candidate must pass certifying exams and demonstrate required experience managing projects. Over the years, an industry has grown up to provide training for exam preparation, and PMI has now certified more than 15,000 PMPs®.

But perhaps PMI made its biggest mark in the project management world when it published *The Project Management Body of Knowledge* in 1987. This publication, which quickly became known as *PMBOK*® (pronounced "pimbok"), became the bible of project management, with in-depth coverage of nine knowledge areas: scope management, cost management, time management, quality management, human resources management, communications management, risk management, contract/procurement management, and project management framework (to cover the relationships between project management and the external environment and between project management and general management). In 1996, PMI published an updated version, changing its name to *A Guide to the Project Management Body of Knowledge*, recognizing – so it said – that one document could never cover the entire body of knowledge on project management. PMI published a new edition of the *PMBOK*® *Guide* in late 2000.

PROJECT MANAGEMENT SPREADS ITS WINGS

In the years since its founding, PMI's membership has changed to reflect the inroads project management practices have made into businesses outside of the traditional engineering/construction/military base. Today the majority of members are either in IT professions or in a wide variety of other industries as far afield from the origins of the discipline as insurance and banking.

Taking off in the 1980s and accelerating its pace in the 1990s, project management took the corporate world by storm. Business literature began touting the matrix organization, which featured an overlay of projects on top of a traditional operations structure. In a matrix, project teams form, drawing their members from functional units and releasing them back into those units when the project is complete and the team disbands. While there may have been more hype than successful matrix reorganization in the 1980s, by the close of the century, the concept of project-based organizations had taken root. By the late

1990s the focus of much project management literature had changed from how to manage one project to how to manage an organization by projects.

TOOLS KEEP PACE

In the 1960s, the only project management software programs that existed were cumbersome and complex systems for mainframes. It took teams of experienced operators to run them, and they were so expensive only the largest companies could afford them. With the advent of the personal computer in the 1980s, there was a demand for project management software as inexpensive and easy to use as word processors, and the software developers did their best to respond. It wasn't long before project management software prices dropped from hundreds of thousands of dollars to a few hundred dollars. Not only could software accessible to anyone automate the charts that were cumbersome to draw by hand, but it could perform modeling functions, allowing project managers to test out "what ifs": If I change this task or that schedule, how will it affect my final outcome?

And, as corporations began talking about managing by projects, software responded by addressing the need to organize and track not just one project but many, with overlapping resources.

In fact, software became so powerful that by the end of the millennium the literature felt the need to remind users not to expect Microsoft Project or other programs to manage their projects for them. Software can sequence tasks, but it can't determine what tasks are worth doing. It can do cost estimates, but it can't judge whether the costs represent value or not. It can create a responsibility assignment matrix, but it can't identify the best people to do the job.

As a new century begins, it's still people, not machines, that manage projects.

MILESTONES IN PROJECT MANAGEMENT

» **1917**: Henry Gantt introduces the Gantt Chart, a scheduling tool still used today.

» **1942–46**: The Manhattan Project uses planning, scheduling, and tracking techniques that became models for future military and industry projects.

» **1958**: The Polaris Missile Program spawns more tools for project managers including the PERT Chart. About the same time, Du Pont and Rand Remington Univac develop the Critical Path Method. The two sequencing tools become jointly known as PERT/CPM.

» **1960s–70s**: The Apollo Space Project becomes a model for the matrix organization and refined methodologies for managing contracts and tracking and controlling project work.

» **1965**: In Europe, a group of project management practitioners form an organization called INTERNET, later changed to International Project Management Association, which has developed into a worldwide network of national project management associations.

» **1969**: The Project Management Institute is born in the United States. Later, chapters formed around the world and it has become the largest project management organization, with a membership of over 75,000.

» **1980s–90s**: Project management outgrows its engineering/construction/military origins and moves into both manufacturing and white-collar industries. Project management software makes the leap from complex and expensive mainframe applications to PC software packages at a price and user-friendliness that make them accessible to all potential users.

» **1984**: PMI certifies the first Project Management Professionals (PMP®).

» **1987**: PMI publishes *The Project Management Body of Knowledge* (*PMBOK®*). Subsequent editions in 1996 and 2000 are known as the *PMBOK® Guide*.

» **2000–2001**: As the new century rolls in, the emphasis has changed to an organization-wide emphasis on managing by projects across entire companies.

NOTES

1 Wideman, R. M., *Project Management Institute: In the Beginning*...
www.maxwideman.com.
2 Wideman, R. M., *Project Management Institute: In the Beginning*...
www.maxwideman.com.
3 (1996) *A Guide to the Project Management Body of Knowledge*,
1996 edn. Project Management Institute, Newtown Square, PA.

The E-Dimension

» What e-tools can do for project managers and teams
» Why everyone is not enamored of them
» How networks support project work
» The move to virtual project teams
» e-Speed: the key to Internet projects

Depending upon your point of view, electronic communication represents either a giant step forward for project management or a dangerous threat to the human relationships that underscore all successful projects.

One thing is certain; the proliferation of dot.coms in the late 1990s created an explosion of new project management opportunities. And even after the burst of the dot.com bubble, earth-bound companies are still keeping IT project managers up to their necks in Web projects. This chapter will take a look at the special challenges and opportunities of Web projects later, but first it will address the impact of e- on traditional project management.

THE TOOLS THAT BIND...OR DIVIDE

Certainly there is a dazzling array of new tools out there that were unheard of only a decade ago. With the tapping of a few keys and the click of a mouse, users can enjoy sophisticated capabilities for:

» sharing accessibility to a project's planning, scheduling, and tracking tools and reports;
» disseminating information to project team members, management, customers, and vendors;
» sharing files among project team members;
» communicating and collaborating with far-flung project team members;
» building and accessing a repository of historical information on an individual project or on projects throughout the enterprise;
» creating and accessing a combined schedule of all projects throughout the enterprise.

On the other hand, those very tools make it possible for people on the same team to avoid ever seeing each other or outside stakeholders face-to-face. To the critics, this is dehumanizing and demotivating, dulling the prospects for breakthrough team problem-solving or creative synergy. Furthermore, without opportunities to read body language, hear voice tone, and volley questions and answers, e-messages are dangerously susceptible to misunderstanding.

Still, not even the most wary of e-critics are saying, "Sever the networks!" They're just reminding us that networks are a tool, not a culture, and that the key to successful project management still lies in building effective personal relationships. That requires getting everyone together in one room periodically, formal and informal one-on-ones with project team members, visiting customers and vendors in person, and – at the opposite end of the spectrum – writing occasional personal letters of appreciation and sending them snail mail. But all those meetings and correspondences can be enhanced and made more productive when data is shared in advance and outcomes are confirmed electronically afterward.

TAKING PROJECT MANAGEMENT ONLINE

LANs

In the beginning was the LAN (Local Area Network). When organizations began to put a computer on every desk in the 1980s, they quickly looked for a way to link up all those stand-alone units. LANs allowed them not only to share software, but also to communicate among computer users in a building or complex. Despite the misgivings noted above, the intent was to unite people, not to separate them. Software like Lotus Notes® gave capabilities like e-mail, document sharing, group discussions, and calendaring and scheduling to LANs (and WANs [Wide Area Networks], which broaden the geographical limits of organizations' networks). Coming at the same time as project management software for PCs, networking made it possible to share project information electronically among team members and others in the organization with a stake in the work of the project.

Intranets

In the 1990s, Internet technology got too good to resist, so organizations began to use it to develop networks of their own. Intranets, which don't need to be connected to the Internet at all, have all the graphic interfaces, hypertext links, and ease of use that make the World Wide Web so appealing to everyone, but are exclusive to the employees of an individual enterprise. With project management now speeding its expansion into white collar and manufacturing sectors, project teams began to create their own Web pages on their company intranets, both for sharing information within the team, and for educating the whole enterprise about what they were doing. Project teams that once would have labored away in obscurity now increased their visibility with regularly updated Web pages aimed at the rest of the organization and intended to build support for their work and anticipation for their deliverables.

Increasingly, organizations are creating central project offices to coordinate the work of all projects across the enterprise. For such an office, an intranet is a perfect location for a unified project calendar and for a repository of historical information on projects throughout the enterprise. Such a repository allows project managers to reap the benefits of past experience instead of reinventing wheels.

Extranets

But even intranets have their limitations; they're accessible only to connected computers (although dial-in access can be provided, but even that is restricted, since the whole point of an intranet is to keep it within the family). For communication, collaboration, and commerce with their partners, customers, and vendors, organizations took to the Internet itself, building extranets, password-protected communities that know no geographical, hardware, or company boundaries. With projects going global, outsourcing components to outside providers, and often working in close collaboration with their customers, extranets provide a medium for:

» cooperating among colleagues at worldwide locations for planning and tracking project work;
» sharing information such as contracts, milestones, schedules, deliverables, status reports, key decisions, and outstanding issues with customers and other outside stakeholders – project managers can decide what to share with whom;
» getting sign-offs on deliverables, documents for review, and changes from customers and stakeholders;
» online discussions among everyone concerned about deliverables, changes, and issues.

THE RISE OF THE VIRTUAL PROJECT TEAM

If you were building a dam in the 1930s, you hired people to work exclusively on your project until the dam, or at least their part of it, was done. If you were developing a breakthrough minicomputer in the 1970s, as Tracy Kidder vividly described in his book, *The Soul of a New Machine*, you brought people together in a basement somewhere to devote themselves to your project 18 hours a day until it was done. But in the early twenty-first century, a typical project manager may be charged with a very different kind of task, such as developing an information management system for an insurance company with nation-wide operations. If you are that kind of project manager, you are probably working through a team of people assigned to your project part-time, who represent a range of business interests and are located in offices around the country.

These days, the virtual project team, composed of people separated by vast distances who communicate primarily by computer and telephone, is more the norm than the exception. For them, e-communication is not an alternative to face-to-face, it's the only way they can operate. They use networks to develop a sense of community among project team members who may be far-flung geographically and to keep channels open to various regional and functional units that can contribute to the project or be impacted by it. Network-enabled project software helps virtual project teams plan and track progress of widely dispersed project components, keep the various components in sync with each other, manage project change across the board, and deter local scope changes from overwhelming the project.

It's not a question of people on a project team e-mailing each other instead of walking down the hall or driving across town to talk in person. It's a question of using electronic means to take advantage of the skills, knowledge, and input of people who would not be accessible to the project any other way.

E-BUSINESS PROJECTS

The electronic revolution not only changed the way projects are run, it also spawned a new kind of project, one with significantly different needs and priorities. All those electronic advances don't happen in a business-as-usual environment. They are the result of projects.

With its roots in engineering and math, the computer community has always had a project mentality. Whether for building new hardware or developing software, the approach is to start with a specific goal, a dedicated team, a deadline, and whatever resources are available – from the legendary garage and a shoestring budget to the Microsoft billions. Hardware and software projects survive by their ability to balance the three tradeoffs that raise the tension on any kind of project: time, cost, and quality.

THE BIG DIFFERENCE

Internet-related projects are different. On an e-project, time is the overriding priority. That's as true for the development of a glitzy Website as it is for the deployment of a small but technically exquisite applet (for those of us who are Web-challenged, that's a small application we never have to worry about but can be glad is there helping us surf). Pundits liken the explosion of Internet technology to the gold rush: if you don't stake your claim quickly, you'll be left in the dust.

So what are the tradeoffs? Well, your finances may be limited or all the money in the world may not speed up the creative muse. So, by the standards of other kinds of projects, if something has to be sacrificed, it's quality. Accepted procedure is: get something out there and fix it later.

Customers have come to accept, even to demand, this new reality. They wouldn't buy a car without doors or headlights and wait for those features to come in a "patch." But they'll eagerly grab new Internet technology before it's clean of all glitches, let alone been gussied up with bells and whistles. And the demise of the dot.coms hasn't slowed down the expansion of the World Wide Web. From small home businesses to multibillion-dollar corporations to municipal governments, the Web is the place to be now – if not yesterday – even if it's just with a basic site that permits add-ons later.

Because of this emphasis on time, e-projects:

» require brutal resistance to scope change: "Let's just add this one thing. It won't take long and it will make everything work better."

E-project teams are as full of good ideas as anyone, but the standard operating answer is "No. We'll go to market with what we've got and add that later."

» are iterative, rather than discrete. Viewed this way, an e-project never ends, since each release spawns a continuum of new releases to make the improvements that were left out the first time.

CRITERIA FOR SUCCESS

Getting to market at warp speed may force a project to lower other priorities, but there are two additional criteria that no project can sacrifice and still succeed.

» *Ease of use*. The outcome doesn't have to be perfect, but it does have to work. And, increasingly, it has to be easy enough for a techno-novice to use.
» *Security*. There's a lot of very private information moving through the Internet and there are some terrifying examples of that information being stolen. Even the race to market can't allow a product or service to compromise the user's online security.

THRIVING IN AN E-WORLD

Internet technology is changing so fast that managing any e-project is like throwing darts at a moving target. Project managers in other fields who use Internet technology to help them manage their projects experience similar effects. Just as they learn to get the most out of one electronic tool, there's a new one out there enticing them to switch or to add another layer. It's dizzying, and it's not going to slow down. As developers or users, we'll all be riding this roller coaster for a long time to come.

E-LESSONS FROM A CUTTING-EDGE COMPANY

When you are a project manager in a leading technology services firm, you learn fast to make the most of electronic advances. Three project managers in such a company shared lessons they learned managing the development of Websites and a systems maintenance project that affected every computer and application throughout the company's worldwide offices. Here's what they said.

» Use e-mail vociferously to stay in contact with all team members and stakeholders, but do not use it to replace human contact. You still need regular face-to-face meetings, or at least teleconferences if your team is geographically dispersed.
» Use the company intranet to keep the entire enterprise informed and engaged. That way you'll have a willing and knowledgeable base to draw from if you need to pull more people into your project later.
» Put your planning and scheduling tools and report templates online so dispersed team members can access them.
» On an e-project, there is never enough time, but you have to meet your promised launch date anyway. So identify the bare essentials and stick with those for the first iteration.
» An e-project is a constant process of learn, launch, learn, adapt, relaunch, learn, adapt, relaunch... Listen to your users and adapt to meet their needs in future iterations.
» On a Website project, involve your potential audience from the outset. You'll save time, money, and audience loyalty if you gear your first iteration to your users' key needs and wants.
» Make your Website user-friendly from the start, even if that means – as it did for one team – a week of 24-hour days solving a usability problem discovered just before launch.
» Websites require teams of people from very different fields: business, technology, graphic arts, marketing, editorial, financial. One of the project manager's crucial responsibilities is to see that they all understand each other. These project managers found on several occasions that what appeared to be an insurmountable obstacle was a translation problem, not a resource one.

The Global Dimension

» Nortel Network's route to global project management
» Recommendations for setting global project management standards
» Culture shock: the people side of going global
» A model for understanding cultural differences
» How to help expatriates and locals understand each other better

Imagine yourself working for an enterprise with projects around the world. You provide a range of products and services for customers in more than 100 countries. Some of your customers are as global as you are, and for those customers your company has projects in several locations. Now imagine that all those projects are using project management processes and tools selected by their individual project managers, who come from a variety of disciplines and have varying amounts of formal project management training.

You've just imagined yourself into the real-life scenario of a lot of very big companies.

But, sooner or later, someone in your organization is going to start asking why Project Team A in Country B is so much more efficient than Team B in Country D. And one of those repeat customers is going to wonder why working with your firm in Country C is so different from working with your firm in Country A.

Inevitably those questions are going to lead the people in your company to start talking about global project management. About implementing consistent processes and tools for all projects around the world. About building a system that can integrate scheduling and resource allocation internationally. About installing project management software with a central database and Web-enabled accessibility for everyone.

Lots of companies are talking about global project management. Just how many are actually doing something about it hasn't been well documented yet. There are critics in the literature who suggest that global project management is actually a little like the weather: everybody talks about it but no one does a thing about it. That is a harsh judgment. In fact, there is a growing trend among organizations operating internationally to build standardized project management systems for their global operations.

One company that's doing that is Nortel Networks, one of the world's leading providers of telecommunications products, including switching, wireless and broadband systems for service providers; residential and business telephones and systems; fiber-optic networks; and Internet Protocol networking technologies. Nortel Networks has headquarters offices in Canada and the United States and regional offices around the world.

A CUSTOMER-DRIVEN CHANGE

When Nortel Networks' Bill Marshall first got the inspiration to standardize the way the company managed its customer-facing projects, Nortel Networks was organized around products. There was, for example, a group that built and sold switches, another for wireless, and another for telecommunications enterprise products. As long as the various product groups worked independently of each other, it didn't seem to matter that they worked differently. But as the telecommunications industry matured, customers began asking not for individual products but for total communications solutions, involving all Nortel Networks' product lines.

Nortel Networks responded by bringing in experts from various parts of the organization to meet with the client. Sometimes it was painfully obvious even to the customer that these people were meeting each other for the first time and that there was no consistency in the way they approached projects.

In that environment, Marshall, who now heads up Nortel Networks' Global Markets Project Management Core Team, relocated to Richardson, Texas after working in the Asia-Pacific area where he had been in charge of telecommunications projects. After his experience there, Marshall had a mission: to establish consistent standards in project management for the organization.

At about the same time, the corporation recognized the need to coordinate events and services throughout the company and approached the issue from a slightly different angle, turning to supply chain management for a solution. Teams went into action to identify the business processes, discover the integration points where those processes interacted, and understand what data had to pass from one process to the other at those points. The first outcomes were diagrams of nearly 20 processes, but no way to coordinate them from end to end.

By then, Marshall's team had begun its work at standardizing project management. The team now recognized the even bigger implications of what they were doing. Mike Bickel, who is responsible for market project management standard implementation, says, "We realized it was project management that would tie the processes together from end to end."

He explains, "Our process requires that the sales force engage the project management organization early, when they are first putting together the proposal. They use the project manager to do a risk assessment and start on a project plan that will satisfy customer requirements." The project management process also covers procurement of all parts – whether manufactured by Nortel Networks or obtained from third party vendors; delivery, installation, and testing of products; training of customers in their use, and ultimately obtaining a sign-off that the work has been done.

GOING GLOBAL

Project management oversight of the supply chain process caught on in Nortel Networks' North American operations before it went global. But in late 1999, Nortel Networks reorganized, moving from a product-based organization to a geographically based one with six regions – United States, Canada, Latin America, Brazil, Asia-Pacific, and EMEA (Europe, Middle East, Africa). In each region, someone at the director level was made responsible for the market project management processes and charged with serving as a liaison to the Core Team in Richardson. The team worked with these regional representatives to standardize project management around the world.

"Part of our strategy," Bickel says, "was to get these people involved in all our decisions." The regional directors formed a Process Council, who voted on all standardization decisions. "In most cases, decisions were unanimous," Bickel says. "Very few people ever said no to a recommendation. Instead they'd say, 'Well, in addition we'd like...' after working that out everyone would support the decision. That Process Council was really the key to getting global buy-in and support."

HOW THE SYSTEM WORKS

With that global support, Nortel Networks installed standardized automated project management tools, using Open Plan software, integrated with an Oracle database. One of its features is that the system takes financial data from contract ledgers and project schedule input by project managers and combines them in Open Plan tools that do cost and schedule performance measurements, comparing estimates to actuals.

Along with providing standard tools, the Core Team is also standardizing practices, by combining the best of what was happening spontaneously throughout the regions. On a Website, the Core Team posts best practices in two categories: There is an approved list and there is another list that contains suggestions for people to try. After suggestions have been on the second list for a while, the Process Council votes on them. Either they make it onto the approved list or they get dropped.

Approved best practices that have come from the field include a communications plan, responsibility assignment matrix, project close report, risk analysis tool, project binder, baseline change request, and invoice-triggering template.

"The core team wouldn't have thought of these," Bickel says, "but as people in the field come up with good ideas, we encourage other people to try them, then make a standard, rather than have everyone doing something different.

"We really discourage people from doing things on their own," he adds. "We won't support development money for processes that aren't approved."

TRAINING FOR USERS

To help project managers around the world make the most of the standard processes and new tools, Nortel Networks has provided three types of training.

First, members of the Core Team have visited the regions and conducted classes. The primary one is a "Walk-the-Wall" session. They put a flow diagram of the new process on the wall and have the attendees identify gaps between their current process and the new one, and then identify actions to eliminate the gaps. The Core Team members usually describe the automated system architecture and give a fundamental class on the use of Open Plan within the architecture.

Second, Nortel Networks contracted with vendors to provide training on the software as well as a series of classes that go from preparation for the PMI PMP® exam to a more complex experienced-based class on multiproject program management.

Third, the Core Team has developed a series of three CDs that contain information regarding the new process, procedures, tools, and metrics.

THE BENEFITS

What's come out of the new system is improved financial management and risk management on projects. Customer approval ratings are increasing too.

Just as important, there is a lot of enthusiasm and buy-in among project managers around the world, largely because the best practices have made it their system, not something forced on them. In the first year the system was up and running, Nortel Networks offered two monthly awards – porcelain eagles that rotated among the winners, one for progress in implementing the global process, the other for offering the most best practices. After a year, the eagles went permanently to the regions that had won them most often. Brazil got one and Asia-Pacific the other.

BEST PRACTICES FOR SETTING GLOBAL STANDARDS

Culled from Nortel Networks' experience, these practices support the successful implementation of global project management:

» Integrate your process with other changes the enterprise is making, such as Nortel Networks' movement into supply chain management. You can capitalize on complementary organizational reforms.
» Bring in regional representation from the outset. You can't set global standards from an ivory tower. You'd miss crucial regional issues, plus your users might resist on principle (and they'd probably be justified).
» Get ongoing input from the users. You get great ideas that way and it makes the system theirs, not yours.
» Provide training for users. This should cover processes and procedures as well as tools.

» Put teeth in how you discourage people from using unapproved tools and techniques. *Equally important, if not more so, reward them for using the standard system.*

» Search out Web-enabled enterprise project management software that can be customized to meet your needs. You'll probably have to integrate more than one product into a system that works for you.

» Make the system as easy as possible to use. Nortel Networks' standardized tools include templates for project plans so the project manager doesn't have to start with a blank screen.

» Build in continuous improvement. Keep the system flexible and open to improvements.

IN THE TRENCHES

So far, this chapter has concentrated on the global dimension of project management from the organizational point of view. There's another side to it, with a different set of issues, that individuals wrestle with when they join a multinational project team, leave home to manage a project on the other side of the world, or play host to project team members from another country. It's the difficulty of getting along, building relationships, understanding others and being understood, in a strange culture. Suddenly, seemingly innocuous gestures and words take on unintended meanings, and actions that worked well in the past have unexpected outcomes where role expectations are totally different.

THE CULTURE CLASH

Harold Kerzner, author of many books on project management and a well-known trainer of project managers, tells a story of an American project manager in Brazil. The American would express approval by making a circle of his thumb and forefinger, signaling A-OK. At least, that's what he thought he was signaling. But to his Brazilian team members, he was making an obscene gesture.

"Sometimes," Kerzner says, "project managers simply don't understand how their actions are interpreted in other countries. Even patting someone on the back may be offensive."

Social gaffes like these can certainly get a visitor off to the wrong foot in a new country. Globe-trotting project team members can easily make mistakes and misunderstand other people's meanings regarding culturally distinctive attitudes toward personal space (How close is too close?), eye contact (respectful or disrespectful?), touching (friendly or unforgivably intimate?), symbolic gestures, or the use of terms. But these are only sparks in the clash of cultures that's almost bound to ensue when a project team from one country takes on an endeavor in another or when a project pulls together members from around the world.

With even small companies forming strategic alliances to move into the global arena and the Internet offering a virtual world with instant access and no borders, global projects are more the norm than the exception. But that doesn't make them easy or predictable.

It's hard enough when project team members speak different languages, have to travel exhausting hours to meet face to face, and telecommute across time zones that wreak havoc on normal work schedules. Then there are varying – sometimes conflicting – government regulations that affect doing business. Even more challenging are the deeply imbedded attitudes and beliefs we absorb, usually unconsciously, as children. These constructs help us understand others within our own culture but create mystifying obstacles to relating to people of other cultures. And despite centuries of travel, relocation, even domination of one culture by another, these national, ethnic, and regional differences still exist.

UNDERSTANDING DIFFERENCES

One of the best ways to unlock the mysteries of cultural variations is through the framework developed by Geert Hofstede of The Netherlands. Hofstede's five Cultural Value Dimensions[1] could be an eye-opener for expatriate project managers struggling to meet the expectations of both the local workers and community and the corporate headquarters back home. The dimensions are:

1 *Power Distance*, defining employees' response to and expectations of those in authority.

   In high power distance cultures, bosses tend to be more autocratic and employees expect to be told what to do. In low power distance cultures, employees expect their bosses to consult with them before making decisions. (Based on research he did in the 1960s and 1970s, Hofstede identified Latin America, France, Spain, and most Asian and African countries as regions with high power distance cultures and the United States, Great Britain, and most northern European countries as low power distance.)

   Imagine how that difference in perspective changes the response to the American management dictum: Don't bring me problems, bring me solutions. In the United States, it's meant to be empowering, assuring employees that their managers respect their problem-solving ability and give them the authority to take corrective actions. But in a high-power distance culture, employees interpret such a management attitude as abandonment and, worse, an invitation to hide, rather than report, problems.

2 *Individualism/Collectivism*, or "Which comes first, me or the team?"

   People in individualistic cultures expect to take care of themselves and make decisions based on their own needs. In collectivist cultures, people value loyalty to the group, base decisions on the group's needs, and expect the group to take care of them. (Among countries with individualistic cultures, Hofstede placed the United States, Canada, France, and South Africa. He identified Japan, Mexico, and Greece, for example, as countries with collectivist cultures.)

   Although they are competitive, individualists do work well together on a team when they perceive the team's goals to be complementary to their own and anticipate that the team's success will contribute to their own advancement. Collectivists identify with the team's goals and cooperate to achieve them.

3 *Masculinity/Femininity*, a measurement of whether people in a culture are motivated more strongly by the more "masculine" goals of achievement, advancement, and recognition or by the more "feminine" pursuits of cooperation, security, and good relationships. (Hofstede rated Great Britain, the United States, and Japan among the

highest on masculinity. Sweden, France, and Indonesia were among the top-ranked countries on the femininity scale.)

If you are chafing at the masculine and feminine labels, the terms may be less politically correct now than they were when Hofstede did his original research back in the 1960s and 1970s, but cultures still exhibit the characteristics the words were used to define.

4 *Uncertainty Avoidance*, an expression of people's comfort in situations where the outcome is unknown.

In cultures that rank high on uncertainty avoidance, people prefer to live by rules and structures that minimize the occurrence of unexpected results. People with low uncertainty avoidance place more value on the opportunity for innovation and creativity than on the assurance of guaranteed results, and may even be energized by the risks inherent in a project with an uncertain outcome. (Hofstede's research placed Korea, Japan, and Latin America high on the uncertainty avoidance scale and the United States, The Netherlands, and Great Britain among those countries on the low end.)

5 *Long-term/Short-term Orientation*, which is about the willingness to make tradeoffs between short- and long-term gratification. (China, Japan, and India rated high among countries having cultures with long-term orientation and Great Britain, Canada, and Germany were among countries with short-term orientation.)

THE MEANING OF TIME

One big cultural divide that's not described in the snapshots of Hofstede's cultural dimensions above is the meaning of "on time." In project management, that's a pretty critical attribute, since project success is usually defined as meeting specifications, on time, and within budget. Yet cultural differences range from "within 30 seconds with no excuses," to sometime within the decade if nothing else comes up. To generalize – even to stereotype – there seems to be a north-south variation here, with northern cultures viewing time more precisely and southern ones taking a more leisurely attitude. For projects that cross through the Tropics of Cancer and Capricorn, it's a good idea to build some extra "float" time into the plan.

IS IT A COUNTRY THING?

So can a project manager click on a country and come up with a list of key cultural attributes that will explain everything? Not hardly. First, even within countries there are regional and ethnic differences. (Within the world's 200+ countries are over 3000 identified ethnic groups.) Neglecting those differences had led to fatal clashes among workers. Second, despite the value of identifying cultural differences, placing too much faith in them can lead to stereotyping, which can be equally dangerous. So there's no easy "when in Rome" solution. But a greater awareness of culture's impact certainly improves every project team's chances for working well together.

WHOSE RESPONSIBILITY IS IT TO ADAPT?

For expatriates

Taking a pragmatic approach, it makes good sense for expatriates to honor local cultural values and practices. To that end, it's a good idea to:

» allow enough time to accommodate local attitudes and practices;
» get training in advance on the region's specific sensitivities around religious practices, hierarchies in business and family (right down to bowing and seating arrangements), personal space, eye contact, attire, speech colloquialisms and gestures, and other behaviors with the potential for misunderstandings;
» recognize all the cultural variations described by Hofstede as valid, healthy perspectives that are equally supportive of personal and organizational growth; and
» anticipate the potential for cultural misunderstandings, assess their impact, and provide for them in the project's risk management.

For locals

While it may be the expatriate's responsibility to make the biggest change, it's equally important to prepare local project team members for what's in store. Their life will be easier and the project will run more smoothly if they receive training in:

» how to anticipate and interpret the behaviors of the outsiders;
» the cultural values of their "guests" and how those values can contribute to project success;
» which aspects of the project plan (cost, schedule, quality) are immutable, and what that means for them; and
» how they can best make their needs known.

NOTE

1 Hofstede, G. (1990) *Culture and Organizations: Software of the Mind*. McGraw-Hill, New York.

The State of the Art

» The re-emergence of the matrix organization to support projects
» How companies use project management to implement strategy
» The role of the project office – and a note of caution
» The emergence of enterprise project management
» What the future holds

The issues causing a buzz in project management circles these days are not about how to do it. The how-to's for managing a project were formulated and validated years ago and, except for the incorporation of powerful project management software, remain pretty much the same. The big issues today are all about the role of project management within the organization.

For a construction company, the role is pretty straightforward. The company wins a bid to erect a building. There's no way to treat that except as a project with clearly defined milestones and a final goal, after which the job is done. So the company assigns people and resources to do the job within specs and by the scheduled completion day (hopefully). When the project is done, that structure is dissolved. With the next project, the process starts again.

But project management methodologies and tools have moved into white-collar businesses and production facilities. There the situation is different. Insurance companies, for example, employ vast numbers of people who provide ongoing administrative, marketing, legal, and other support services. These organizations are discovering the advantage of applying project management not only to new product development, but also to the improvement of internal processes. This raises a number of questions:

» How do you incorporate project management, with its temporary, cross-functional characteristics, into a hierarchical, functional organization structure?
» How can you take advantage of project management to respond faster and more effectively to opportunities and challenges coming from both outside and inside the enterprise?
» How do you assign resources efficiently to projects popping up around the enterprise?
» How do you keep from reinventing the wheel in projects throughout the enterprise?
» Is it efficient to have various project management tools, not compatible with each other, being purchased and used in different parts of the organization?
» How do you take broad advantage of the lessons learned on individual projects?
» Should there be central oversight of all projects?

For some questions, researchers and practitioners are just now seeking and testing potential responses. Others have inspired new ways of working within organizations.

THE ORGANIZATION CHART

In response to the first question, a number of companies are moving intentionally or *de facto* toward a matrix organization – whether or not they call it that.

The matrix is a double-layered structure in which much of the work is done by temporary cross-functional project teams, led by project managers and staffed by experts drawn from functional units headed up by line managers. Consulting and technology companies have used it for years, and companies in other industries had a well-publicized fling with it in the 1980s. But by the end of the decade or early in the 1990s, the struggles over the dual reporting relationships had become too much for many companies, and they moved back into more traditional modes, accompanied by a flurry of articles with names like "The death of the matrix."

With the growing popularity of projects, the matrix has been resurrected, informally sometimes and often without the name. David I. Cleland of the University of Pittsburgh, who is often called the father of project management, explains:

> "The matrix organization has become to a certain extent institutionalized – the way they do things. I've worked with companies that struggled with it because of the apparent contradictions in reporting relationships. But they have advanced to where they may not call it that, but they are doing it."

If it's difficult, why are companies bothering? The answer is that project management holds out the promise of faster and more effective responses to opportunities and challenges coming from both outside and inside the enterprise.

That leads to the second question in the list above: How does a company take advantage of that promise?

THE LINK TO STRATEGY

It's been a long time since any company could get away with thinking, "Well this year has been good; we'll do the same next year." Looking forward to next year or five years from now means anticipating, planning, and creating change, introducing new products or services before the competition gets ahead, installing new technology that, hopefully, won't be obsolete by the time it is fully functional, developing and implementing new processes that respond faster and more effectively to customer concerns. In more and more companies, when the planners reach the stage of creating strategies like these to fulfill the company's vision and goals, they realize they are describing not ongoing work, but projects.

Projects are the means for implementing strategies.

"Strategic management and project management, interdependently linked, provide the framework for preparing the enterprise to deal with its future, and develop and execute survival and growth initiatives in the marketplace," writes Cleland.[1]

Project management methodologies are ideally suited to the task of carrying out strategic initiatives since they include:

» creating a clear scope statement, defining measurable outcomes of the project, in terms of components, quality, and magnitude;
» identifying resources;
» creating a workable plan and schedule and tracking progress;
» estimating time and costs, and tracking actual performance against the estimates;
» communicating regularly with stakeholders to keep them up-to-date and involved;
» managing change; and
» closing down the project when the goals have been met.

These methodologies were designed to speed up product development and reduce time to market, while maintaining cost and quality control. Using them to manage strategic initiatives provides the same benefits while helping to ensure that the initiative remains goal-directed, flexible enough to respond to changing conditions, and front and center in management's range of vision, rather than pushed into the periphery by the tyranny of business as usual.

Using cross-functional project teams to tackle strategic initiatives rather than working through the operations hierarchy keeps the organization nimble and gives it the advantage of more viewpoints and broader expertise available to tackle problems and exploit opportunities as they arise.

In fact, Cleland claims that the impact is even wider, ultimately affecting the culture of the entire enterprise, encouraging greater entrepreneurship at the front line; more sharing of resources, problems, authority, and rewards; increased willingness to discard obsolete ideas; less resistance to change; greater creativity and innovation flowing from the bottom upward; flatter organizational hierarchies, and a greater tendency to challenge the status quo. (For more on Cleland's thinking on the strategy/project management connection, see Key concepts and thinkers in Chapter 8.)

STRATEGIC PLANNING FOR PROJECT MANAGEMENT

While project management has become a powerful tool for strategists, that's only half of the strategy/project combination that holds the interest of leaders in the project management community. "Organizations are finally recognizing that project management is a strategic competency for the company," says Harold Kerzner, a noted author, scholar, and trainer. "Once they view it that way, they begin doing strategic planning for project management. They are asking themselves where they want to be with regard to project management in two or three years."

One organization that has done that is Nortel Networks, whose global system for project management is described in Chapter 5. Strategic planning starts with assessing current capabilities, and Nortel Networks took advantage of its participation in a benchmarking program with 11 other companies to evaluate its own strengths. "We were above average in most categories, but below in some," states Mike Bickel, who is part of the company's Global Markets Project Management Core Team. "Strategically, we want to find ways to improve in categories where we don't think we measure up. You want to be the best possible."

"We use *PMBOK®* as our vision of what project management ought to be," Bickel says. In striving to achieve that vision, Nortel Networks measures its progress against Kerzner's five levels of project management maturity: common language, common processes, singular methodology, benchmarking, and continuous improvement.[2] "We think we're at level three," Bickel said in mid-2001. "We're seeing results from our methodology. Now it's time to look outside and see how to improve."

Out of Nortel Networks' strategic planning for project management have come:

» initiatives for continual process improvement and improving its automated tools;
» development of a new project accounting system, with the cooperation of the company's financial organization and information systems (IS) community;
» initiatives, including training for local project managers, to get people to use optimally the tools and procedures currently available; and
» cost and schedule performance measurements, geared at minimizing the cost to Nortel Networks while maximizing customer satisfaction.

Like Nortel Networks, which is implementing consistent project management systems worldwide, most companies that view project management as a strategic competency are looking for ways to standardize and improve project management across the organization. One approach to doing that is through a project office.

CENTRALIZED SUPPORT AND OVERSIGHT

The term project office isn't new, but the current use of it has evolved in the past several years. As Harold Kerzner points out, the construction industry and aerospace/defense contractors coined it in the 1950s to refer to the management team for a specific project. Now it means something quite different: an office that serves as the focal point of all project management knowledge within a company.

In practice, the responsibilities of the project office vary from company to company. In a large financial services company, all IT projects go through the project office, which provides personnel experienced in project management as well as a standard methodology and tools to use it. Projects in other areas aren't bound by the project office but have learned to lean on it for support, especially since line managers throughout the organization are spending more and more time managing cross-functional projects whether or not they have project management training. So they enlist someone from the project office to guide them through planning, scheduling the project and tracking their progress.

In other companies, especially those that carry out projects for customers, the project office may oversee every project, maintain a database of lessons learned, provide standardized tools, conduct project reviews, and even provide the project managers.

The full range of project office duties can include the following:

» *Developing a project management process for all projects*. Ideally such a process is flexible enough to provide new project managers with easy-to-use planning, scheduling, estimating, and reporting tools and yet sophisticated enough to work for complex, multimillion-dollar initiatives.

» *Developing templates* for the full range of documentation from project charters to status reports.

» *Continually updating and improving* the methodologies and tools.

» *Defining the roles and responsibilities* of project managers and team members.

» *Providing training and mentoring* for project managers. Project office personnel may perform the training, develop it in conjunction with the in-house training staff, bring in outside consultants, or arrange for project managers to attend offsite training programs. Some project offices also provide mentors for fledgling project managers or broker in-house pairings of experienced and inexperienced project managers.

» *Maintaining a project archive and a database of best practices and lessons learned* and encouraging project teams to take advantage of them rather than repeat mistakes and reinvent the wheel.

» *Benchmarking*, identifying best practices in project management both within and beyond the industry in which the company operates. Another important part of this is assessing the company's own practices, comparing them to the benchmarks, and using the information to make improvements.

» *Conducting project reviews and audits*. Typically this is not a policing action, but rather a supporting one. The goal is to identify potential problems before they turn into crises, and assist projects in improving their performance. In the early stages of a project, project office experts often provide valuable guidance. As the project unfolds, the lessons that come out of project reviews can not only help the specific project, but also provide invaluable input into the database of lessons learned.

» *Reviewing the project portfolio*. This goes beyond attending to the needs of individual projects. Some project offices conduct regular review meetings attended by all the project managers, who give status reports on their projects. The most powerful project offices have go/no-go authority over floundering projects.

» *Staffing projects*. While this is far from a universally accepted role of project offices, some organizations are attempting to solve the chronic problem of resource shortage by centralizing the deployment of project personnel. At best, it's a way to level resources across the full range of projects, especially in situations where projects with less strategic importance are hoarding people while others, more relevant to the organization's goals, are understaffed. At worst, giving the project office this role can lead to resistance, turf battles, and pockets of hidden resources throughout the operating units.

» *Selecting and approving new projects*. At the extreme end of project office powers, the office has authority over which projects the organization will or will not undertake. Project offices with this responsibility usually also control the capital budget for projects.

The skeptics

With the potential for so much power residing in one location, project offices aren't unanimously welcomed by everyone in the project management community. Even the skeptics agree there is value in a central support function, but they fear that project offices are usurping the role of individual project managers, thus threatening the environment of entrepreneurship and empowerment that energizes many projects.

Michael W. Newell, author of *Preparing for the Project Management Professional (PMP) Certification Exam* (AMACOM, New York, 2001), sees a danger in giving project offices responsibility for scheduling individual projects:

> "People working on a project start going to the project office instead of the project manager to check their schedules. The next thing you know they make schedule adjustments without contacting their project manager."

He's leery of giving project offices responsibility for cost estimating, too. A project office may have a small group of people who are experts in estimating, but Newell points out:

> "They are a different group from those who have to work on the project and the ones working on it may not have the motivation to meet these estimates."

Despite the apprehension, the popularity of project offices is growing, and with that growth is a developing attitude that project management can have an even larger role in how organizations operate.

ENTERPRISE PROJECT MANAGEMENT

An increasing number of companies have begun to view project management not just as a way to run individual projects or even many projects, but rather as a way to run the enterprise. The *PMBOK®* *Guide* calls this approach "management by projects." In the literature it's usually called "enterprise project management," and there is an increasing body of knowledge dealing with it. An organization that applies it wholeheartedly is known as a "project-based organization."

Enterprise project management involves more than pulling all existing projects under the auspices of a project office. It's more than an overlay of projects grafted on to a traditional, operations-style hierarchy. Rather it is a sweeping change in organizational mindset to a conviction that the entire organization can be run project-style. Paul Dinsmore, *PM Network* columnist and author of *Winning in Business*

With Enterprise Project Management (AMACOM, New York, 1998) describes it this way:

> "Enterprise project management is based on the view that companies can be organized as portfolios of projects, and thus project management is applicable across the organization."[3]

Does that really mean doing away with all ongoing functions? Not exactly. Somebody still has to manage an ongoing payroll, maintain company-wide systems, and perform other regular support services (although an increasing number of companies are outsourcing such activities). The key thing is that these are support services, not the company's reason to exist.

As more companies turn to projects to implement strategic initiatives, they begin to look more carefully at project management methodologies and tools and ask about how these would apply to operations work. Can they turn cycle time improvement into a project, for example? Can they increase customer satisfaction by taking a cross-functional project team approach to each customer's needs? Can they improve their process management by applying project methodologies to process improvement?

Well, you might be asking, can they?

A solution or a catchphrase?

Nobody calls it a panacea, and nobody says it's right for all organizations. In fact, if you want scholarly statistical proof that it works, you'll have to wait. PMI is running a research project to quantify the value of project management. And the cautious members of the project management community are warning: Don't let project management become a catchphrase or this season's management flavor of the month. Project management and project-based organizations have been a way of life in engineering and construction industries for decades, and nobody wants to see the concepts tarnished as a bunch of businesses with very different traditions have a half-hearted fling with them, then toss them aside in favor of some newer trend.

But there is plenty of anecdotal evidence that management by projects works for companies whose success depends upon being in the forefront of change. Companies like Procter & Gamble, Citibank, AT&T, and American Express have been running important parts of their business this way for some time now. EDS is well on its way to becoming a project-driven organization worldwide.

Another organization that is structured to support project management is Johnson Controls' Automotive Systems Group (ASG), which builds complete interiors for automotive vehicles. ASG has more than 200 plants around the world. The company is organized around their future projects and their project systems. Their business model parallels the automotive customers' organizations, and is structured around the automotive vehicle platforms. This organization allows ASG to respond quickly to new business opportunities, and provides a clear link to the customers' organizations.

Additionally, because ASG ships JIT (just in time), in many cases there is an ASG plant for each of the customers' plants. This allows a powerful focus on future programs (groups of related products) since each project manager has a dedicated SDT (Simultaneous Development Team) including a complete manufacturing plant. Additionally, ASG has project-based financial reporting, dedicated engineering, financial and quality personnel. This allows zero ambiguity for responsibility for future program execution and success.

ASG uses a consistent program management system called PLUS (Product Launch System) worldwide. This system is part of a worldwide system referred to as BOS (Business Operating System). The advantage, Kandt says, is that:

> "We have one language, and one management system for evaluating and reviewing programs. We have one way to authorize and fund programs. If you go anywhere in the world and you sit down for a program review you see the same forms, the same timeline structure, the same roles and responsibilities. The PLUS system helps to unify the culture, which is particularly important when you consider the acquisition of new businesses."

Without standard systems, different regions will behave and operate in dissimilar ways.

How to succeed by really trying

Any company that attempts to implement enterprise project management can increase its odds of succeeding by meeting five criteria recommended by Paul Dinsmore. Project management success, he emphasizes, requires high levels of professional qualifications, executive support, authority and control, prestige and influence, and stakeholder management.[4]

Success, he warns, also hinges on the organization's ability to overcome resistance to change. Even when upper management drives the initiative, it can't succeed at implementing enterprise project management by decree. It has to earn the buy-in of the entire organization to make it work. If, as often happens, the movement starts somewhere within pockets of projects operating alongside a predominantly functional structure, then the job of selling it upward and outward is intense.

The good news is that enterprise project management is not an all-or-nothing thing. If you are a project champion operating in one corner of a global company with dozens of operating units and hundreds of thousands of employees, you don't have to conquer the world all at once. Your business unit may be crying out for its own enterprise project management system if it:

» is running several initiatives aimed at creating something new or changing something that already exists;
» requires input from different functions to complete each of those initiatives; or
» depends upon the outcomes of those initiatives for its success.

If that describes your organization and you want to enhance support for those initiatives and improve coordination and oversight among them, then enterprise project management may be in your future.

If you go that way, one of your first steps will probably be to look for a way to deploy a consistent project management methodology and standard tools across all your projects. That begins the search for the Grail of the perfect software to support such a system.

ENTERPRISE PROJECT MANAGEMENT SOFTWARE

For a project-based organization, the ultimate software would:

» store data from all projects in an easily accessible, centralized data-base;
» allow users to analyze trends, needs, and best practices from that data;
» allow that analysis to be done from any level, from individual project manager to someone with responsibility for global oversight;
» include standard project management tools and forms that work better than the variety of products people may be using now; and
» be comprehensive enough for the most sophisticated analysis, yet simple enough for a part-time project person to use.

Such software must combine centralized storage and analysis capa-bilities with Web-based access to tools by relatively unsophisticated users. Every company is also going to want to be able to customize its software to its own particular needs. There are plenty of vendors offering such products and companies that are using them successfully. In the fast-past world of software development, however, this kind of system is still in its adolescence. You can expect developmental leaps in the next few years.

WHAT ELSE CAN YOU EXPECT?

Two of the top thinkers in the field of project management, David Cleland and Hans Thamhain, professor of management at Bentley College in Waltham/Boston, Massachusetts, looked into their crystal balls and shared what they saw there for this book.

Toward a theory

Cleland is looking forward to an overarching theory of project manage-ment. He elaborates:

"Is there a theory of project management? That is an important question. A theory would provide the philosophy and concepts that support and validate the processes of project management.

It's how you think about the discipline. The tools and techniques are how you make it happen.

"There are plenty of books and publications appearing today that deal with how to manage projects. They are good, but we need to build more of a theoretical and conceptual framework. We need to see if there is something really unique about it. So far we are borrowing a lot from general management thought and theory.

"General management is based upon several theories – theories of motivation, for example, like Maslow's Hierarchy of Needs. But we don't yet have anything like that for project management.

"PMI is getting some significant research underway to deal with changes in project management. In June 2000 we had a conference on project management at the millennium. Here is a professional association looking into what research needs to be carried out. To me that is most significant."

A new style of project leadership

Hans Thamhain, whose insights are a major influence on other leading project management teachers and writers, sees a movement in projects away from hierarchical leadership toward a self-directed team-based model. He explains:

"The new generation of project leaders must deal effectively with the new challenges and realities of today's business environment, which include highly complex sets of deliverables, as well as demanding timing, environmental, social, political, regulatory and technological factors. Working effectively in such an intricate environment requires new skills in both project administration and leadership, especially for complex, technology-based and R&D-oriented projects, that rely to an increasing extent on innovation, cross-functional teamwork and decision-making, intricate multi-company alliances and highly complex forms of work integration. Project success often depends to a considerable extent on member-generated performance norms and work processes, rather than supervision, policies and procedures. As a result, self-directed and commitment-based concepts are gradually replacing the traditional more hierarchically structured project organization."[5]

WHAT IS THE STATE OF THE ART?

These are indeed heady times for project management. For years it was a specialty practiced by a few. Now it's gone mainstream and in doing so is changing the way organizations run their businesses. And, as Thamhain says:

"While this shift is enhancing the status and value of project management within the enterprise, it raises the overall level of responsibility and accountability, and puts more demands on project management to perform as a full partner within the integrated enterprise system."[6]

NOTES

1 Cleland, D. I. (1998) "Strategic project management," from *The Project Management Institute: Project Management Handbook* (ed J.K. Pinto). Jossey-Bass, San Francisco.

2 Kerzner, H. (2001) *Strategic Planning for Project Management Using a Project Management Maturity Model*. Wiley, New York. Kerzner's five levels can also be found on www.iil.com.

3 Dinsmore, P. (February, 2000) "Managing projects on an enterprise basis," *PM Network*.

4 Dinsmore, P. (February, 2001) "Enterprise project management: flavor of the day or here to stay," *PM Network*.

5 Quoted from "Project management in a changing world," a working paper by Hans Thamhain, made available through personal correspondence.

6 Quoted from "Project management in a changing world," a working paper by Hans Thamhain, made available through personal correspondence.

In Practice

» How a small project team produced big results
» How a determined project team raced against time to launch a new product
» The story of a mega-project that spanned five years and thousands of miles

Companies are applying project management to a wide variety of endeavors, from short-term, internal initiatives to products for customers that take years to complete. This chapter describes three very different projects: a Website created by people working on it part time and without formal project management training; the development of a new business initiative that was a race against time; and a giant construction project that spanned five years and thousands of miles. The projects are geographically diverse also: one in the United States, one in Germany, and one carried out by a Japanese company in Qatar.

GARTNER ALUMNI CONNECT PROJECT: YOU CAN'T DO IT ALONE

Just months before launch date, Kathleen Warren, vice president of Gartner, the Stanford, Connecticut-based technology services firm, took over a semi-stalled project to create a corporate alumni program – later named Gartner Alumni Connect. The project had the sponsorship of the CEO, who conceived of it as a way to showcase Gartner to former employees and build them into a network of goodwill ambassadors for the company. At its heart would be an alumni Website, and therein lay the rub. At the very same time, a much larger Gartner project team was in the process of building a new corporate Website intended to spearhead a business transformation for the company, providing its clients with vastly increased access to online services. What that meant for Warren was that there just weren't any in-house people with Web skills left to work on her project.

She wasn't left entirely on her own. Julie Viscardi, who reported to the head of human resources, sized up the situation and asked her boss to free her up to help Warren. "What started as 'I'll help you as much as I can,' became full-time as we got to launch date," Viscardi recalls. Warren delegated to her such tasks as site testing, resolving data privacy issues, and database management. That allowed Warren to focus on getting the site launched and making sure the content was appropriate to the audience.

Warren and Viscardi pulled off an award-winning result, on time and within their $500,000 budget, but they had to leverage their own time carefully (which admittedly often meant working extremely long hours) and go to outside sources for the technical talent they needed. And that led to problems down the line they did not anticipate.

The first surprise

At the outset, they were caught up in solving a problem no one had anticipated. The first project manager had quit the company suddenly. When Warren took over, she discovered the project was not nearly as far along as anybody thought. In fact she was starting from scratch. Warren and Viscardi mitigated that problem with hard work and long hours. They also leveraged Warren's 12-year tenure with the company to take advantage of her network of in-house colleagues and former colleagues who had moved on. That helped them get the massive amount of information they needed to ensure the program would meet users' needs.

Getting audience buy-in

The program they were developing was aimed at 4500 Gartner alumni dispersed around the world, so Warren and Viscardi made getting their audience's input and buy-in top priority. To reach these people, they started with the network of contacts Warren had built up in her years with Gartner. Via her network and the contacts of other highly tenured Gartner employees, they connected with a broad, international group of former Gartner people, many of whom had been with Gartner for many years and were still shareholders.

Warren and Viscardi reached out to their potential customers in some exceptional ways, including hosting dinners for groups in both the United States and the United Kingdom. They found out what people wanted and what they didn't want. Keep it primarily e-based, the alumni said, although they also liked the idea of sponsored events to draw people together. But they emphatically did not want to get lots of mail (postal) or fat alumni directories. They wanted to be able to search the alumni Website for their former friends and colleagues, but they also wanted tight control over their own profiles in the database. People in the international regions in particular have very strong ideas on privacy, Viscardi discovered. They wanted to say whether or not they would be in the database and what information about themselves ("just their e-mail address or all about their five kids") would appear if they self-selected to be there. Warren and Viscardi built all of these functional preferences into the program.

The alumni they met with had other, highly practical requests too. They asked for discounts at Gartner conferences. Gartner Alumni Connect responded by offering free tickets to some conferences to alumni who met certain criteria. Everyone Warren and Viscardi talked to requested free access to research on www.gartner.com. That, too, they built into the program, again with eligibility requirements, even though they realized it could cost the company significant dollars.

Inter-team liaison

Warren and Viscardi were building the alumni Website at the same time as a much larger project was underway to completely redo the corporate Website. The plan was always for gartner.com to "adopt" the alumni site, once the main site was up and running smoothly. It was up to Warren and Viscardi to ensure that their Website was in sync with the larger one. "Both we and our vendors had to be sure that whatever we did short-term could be supported internally long-term," Viscardi explains. "If not, we wouldn't be able to offer it. We had to have two sign-offs all the time."

So Warren and Viscardi communicated frequently with the individuals supporting the gartner.com group. Sometimes it was hard to get their time, Viscardi recalls, but she and Warren persevered. "We'd say, 'This is what we're going to do. Can you support it?' A week later we'd get a yes or no."

On the plus side

Because her project was the brainchild of the company's CEO, Michael Fleisher, Warren was in a unique situation. Access to top management was a lot easier than it often is for project managers toiling away on something obscure. Because he was passionate about the project, Fleisher spent considerable time with Warren when she took it on, articulating his vision and explaining his objectives. With the tight project schedule and the CEO's personal interest, Warren didn't need the discipline of regularly scheduled monthly meetings to get his attention as work on the project progressed, nor could she assume such a schedule would be adequate. Instead, via face-to-face contact or e-mail when necessary, she kept him regularly updated on the functionality of the site, deadlines, timelines, etc. The weight of the CEO's name helped expedite many issues that could have stalled the project. But that was a tool Warren and Viscardi tried to use judiciously to avoid causing resentment.

On the other hand, the CEO's avid interest also meant the pressure was intense, as was the scrutiny. The CEO had already had one unpleasant surprise when the first project manager left the company and he discovered how little had been done on the project.

This time, there could be no such surprises.

As the months passed, it looked as if, despite the early problems, the new Website was in great shape.

And, then, a hitch

It was a week before the scheduled launch date when Warren and Viscardi discovered bugs in the program. The "tangled web of vendors," as Viscardi describes them, blamed each other. The problems at that stage weren't big – one was with the time/date stamp – but they were enough that the team could imagine site visitors snorting, "Gee, they gave us something and it doesn't even work." That kind of reaction wasn't going to contribute to the community of good will the project was created to develop.

First corrective step: Delay the launch one week. They could do that and stay within the promised timeframe. That let them buy a little time.

But, says Viscardi, a big problem was that she and Warren just couldn't communicate with the vendors in the technical language necessary to get a grip on the issues. Unfortunately for them, all the people at Gartner with the right expertise were working on creating the new corporate Website. So, Viscardi recalls, "I went to the CIO and begged for help."

And help she got. The CIO lent the project his best troubleshooter, Kevin Volpe, whose regular job was managing the group that solves clients' technical problems, not internal ones. After Gartner's head of networking figured out the problem the Friday before the new Monday launch date, Volpe and his group worked round the clock over the weekend to fix the site.

The site launched that Monday, looking great to visitors. But for the Gartner team the problems hadn't ended. With Warren now off on sabbatical, Viscardi discovered quickly that the site did not automatically register users the way they'd expected. Instead she had to input user information manually. Buried under the volume, by the end of the first week she was again begging the CIO for help. Volpe took the problem off her hands by having his group assume the task of registering users and answering their questions.

They saved the project through heroic efforts, and the company honored them for it. Warren, Viscardi, and Volpe won a coveted Silver Award. Warren received the prestigious Gold Award from the CEO and a promotion. Viscardi moved into a new job she loves, managing Gartner Alumni Connect full-time.

NEXT TIME...

Without professional project management training, the small core team on this project succeeded by hard work, determination, good relationships, top-level support, and the ability to learn as they went along. Julie Viscardi was forthright about disclosing what she'd do differently another time:

» *Anticipate the unwelcome outcomes of a project.* "I think it would be more helpful documenting all the different scenarios that could occur and having a back-up plan in place just in case those scenarios came into reality."

» *Do more homework on the vendors.* "The vendors we ended up using, in hindsight, were probably not the best choice." Later, after the launch problems, she considered using another vendor. By that time she was working closely with the CIO's group, who gave her forms to fill out that called for 12 pages of detail. "Painful as it is, it would have been nice to have done this ahead of time," Viscardi says. "I would have been more prepared. It provokes your thinking and forces you to confront things you might not have thought of."

» *Spread the word internally.* Viscardi realized later that, by working exclusively with outside vendors, they were limiting insider knowledge of their project. That made her job more difficult when, as a last resort, she had to find in-house help to breach the communications gap with the vendors and solve site problems that arose. If she could do it again, Viscardi says, she'd spend more time educating internal associates, "so when we called upon any one group for help, they would have had a firm idea of the program, its objectives, and timelines to launch the Website."

SIEMENS' MTS WEB HOSTING PROJECT: A TRIUMPH OF TEAMWORK OVER TIME

Pressured by time and propelled by teamwork, a project team at Siemens Business Services GmbH & Co OHS (SBS) took just nine months to deliver a new business capability for the company: automated Web hosting.

Until 2000, the German company, which provides electronic and mobile business solutions and services, had concentrated its Web hosting business on the made-to-order market. It engineered each system to the customer's specifications. In January 2000, SBS' Operations Services group commissioned the MTS Web Hosting project. This project's purpose was to develop an automated "made-to-stock" (MTS) product, a standardized interface for setting up, managing, administering and controlling Web hosting service and systems. The company saw the potential for expanding its business in this field.

SBS named a project sponsor, who represented management, and a project director that January and charged them with pulling together a team and completing the project by October 1 of that year. The company created a steering committee to provide oversight. As the project progressed, the company also commissioned two subprojects, one to set up a call center and one to develop the billing process, to take some of the pressure off the project team.

The challenges

Even supported by the subprojects, the MTS Web Hosting project team had a very short time to pull off such an initiative. Compounding that challenge were other factors:

» The technology was complex and had to be interwoven with existing SBS infrastructure and the Internet.
» The project began with a virtual team, who did project work "on the side." Members worked out of their own offices and remained responsible for their other, full-time jobs.
» The full-time project team, appointed part-way through the project, did not come together in one location until July, when the team moved into its own office in Fürth.
» A company reorganization coincided with the Web hosting launch date and changed the direction of the final product.

At a glance, these circumstances seemed ordained to keep people apart rather than bring them together. Nevertheless, what defined the project and led to its success was a focus on teamwork, meeting the needs of team members, and motivating them to be innovative and act on their own initiative.

Building the team

Faced with a complex job in a compressed timeframe, Wolfgang Rzehak, the project director, first pulled together a virtual team, consisting of himself, a deputy project manager, staff members who remained in their own departments, and a part-time external consultant. (In SBS terminology, the consultant was called the project manager, while Rzehak, the internal person who had accountability for the project, was called the project director.) This group's task was to draw up a project business plan. After the business plan was approved in April, work began on staffing a full-time project team.

When it was complete, the team consisted of a Web designer, communication manager, navigator, programmer, sales and marketing manager, chief technology officer, and customer care manager (head of the call center subproject), as well as the program director. Some members of the final team had participated in the virtual team. Others were recruited from throughout the company to fill specific needs for skills and expertise. SBS retained the external project manager and brought in a project assistant from outside. The project also recruited four students from universities and technical colleges, offering them hands-on training or final-year project work. Over the course of the project, about 30 other SBS people joined up for temporary stints to contribute specialized expertise.

To boost team members' skills, SBS arranged specific training in the critical Internet technologies. To broaden their knowledge, they had access to research by providers like Gartner. As time went on, they shared their new expertise with each other at weekly team meetings, called "JourFix."

Team members needed crash courses in project management too, but, says Rzehak, there was no time to send them to classes. Instead, the external project manager led on-the-job training in such topics as project planning, controlling and reporting, and using Microsoft Project™, which is the SBS standard for project management software.

But building a team involves more than skill development. Relationships are the glue that holds a team together, bonding it into a medium for extraordinary results. While it put a lot of effort into building skills, the MTS Web Hosting team put as much – if not more – effort into building relationships among team members, between management and team, and between the team and other stakeholders. In the days before the team was housed together in one office, that was a challenge.

A new kind of leadership

One of the first issues that arose was the team's response to the project director's leadership style. Although Rzehak had made clear at the outset that he expected team members to take initiative and act on their own authority, this was a new way of working for some team members and they were uncomfortable with it. What they wanted, says Rzehak, was "an open door policy and clear feedback if there were problems." So he did things as the team wanted, and it worked.

The team assumed decision-making responsibilities. Changes in the automation process, team communication, and the master plan all came out of team brainstorming sessions. "My task was in most ways a political task," explains Rzehak, "to talk to other managers in our organization (SBS) and the entire Siemens organization."

Team development

The JourFix turned out to be a good place to air any conflicts or disagreements that arose during the course of the project. The team learned to use a decision support matrix when differences of opinion arose. When the issues were clear on paper, Rzehak found, the solutions became clearer too, and the different parties would "be going the same way after a short discussion."

Oddly enough, the time pressure sometimes helped, subduing the urge to argue over minor points. When time is tight, Rzehak points out, "simple things like definitions aren't in discussion over days."

But by mid-summer conflicts had erupted over who was responsible for what, exacerbated by the intense time pressure. Rzehak decided to use the external consultant to lead the team in openly discussing their problems. After two team-building sessions, the problems were solved and team morale strengthened. It was a change in attitude the company was able to measure by conducting two surveys of team members, one in June and one after the team disbanded in December.

With the move into the team's own office space in mid-summer, team members were together full-time at last. Separated from the main buildings and enjoying redecorated rooms and workplaces, good team meeting places, and even a very nice kitchen, the team truly gelled and work progressed rapidly.

Branding also helped the team coalesce. The Web hosting product was named "Yucee" and can be found at www.yucee.de. "The name was a big point in team identity," asserts Rzehak. "We produced shirts, caps, cups, ballpoints. Yucee is a fantasy name and means 'you will see' (against all problems)."

Communication – an essential ingredient

You can't have a successful team effort without outstanding communication processes, both within the team and with outside stakeholders. The Web Hosting team developed a communication program that expanded as the project moved along.

At the heart of the process were the weekly JourFixes. Every Monday at 9 a.m., the core team met to deliver work progress reports, communicate successes and discuss difficulties, submit change requests when appropriate, reassess goals as necessary, and plan for the upcoming week.

There were also wider team meetings with members of the subprojects and additional staff brought in to handle temporary assignments.

In addition, the project director and other team members met regularly with potential customers and partners to make presentations about the project and discuss possibilities for cooperation.

That wasn't always easy. When the project team developed a model using new kinds of servers and the LINUX operating system, people in operations objected, protesting that they were unfamiliar with the hardware and software. Because they needed the agreement of the rest of the organization to proceed, the project team initiated subteams, bringing together team members and representatives from operations. The goal was to understand each other and educate the organization about the team's efforts.

The ability to access information electronically evolved as the project developed. Initially, each contributing department maintained its own project files. Soon, however, the project team set up its own information management system, which was systematically reviewed by the project director, communications manager, and the team members as necessary. Ultimately, data were saved on a shared drive on a central computer, allowing access by all team members by password.

The team also had a secure Internet site, www.teamplace.de, where not only team members but also other authorized stakeholders could view selected files and the project plan. This Website was a Siemens prototype that the MTS Web Hosting team used in a beta version. Finally, to keep interested Siemens personnel up to date, project updates appeared on the company intranet.

Evolution of processes

The staff grew as a team, communications developed into a sophisticated and comprehensive system, and project management processes became more focused and better defined as the project progressed. At the beginning, the team worked with an enormous master plan. After about four months the plan had become overwhelming, with over 600 work packages. That's when the team split off some of the work into the two subprojects. And responsibility for the individual work packages went to the people carrying them out, who reported back on their progress at each JourFix. The project director was responsible for coordinating the packages. The external project manager handled the task of documenting the project plan and changes to it.

The project began by using a project management process based on the company's existing quality management system. But the team was open to trying new processes that could help project implementation. In June, through internal benchmarking the team identified and began using a prototype project management system developed in another SBS project. The two projects regularly exchanged know-how, helping to avoid errors in using the new system.

Results

By the scheduled delivery date, October 1, 2000, "Yucee" was ready for market, although it had changed somewhat from its original design. The project's final challenge was to handle a budget cut and change in direction mandated by management after a company reorganization. Conceived as a Web hosting package for small and medium-sized businesses, the product now was to be automated Web hosting for large companies.

As it had done for months, the team confronted this new challenge and met its new goal, fulfilling the purpose of developing a new business opportunity for SBS – and did so on time and within budget. Management assessed the outcome as "very good," and the demand for MTS Web Hosting exceeded original expectations.

"YUCEE" LESSONS

Since Yucee means "You will see," it is appropriate to use it to describe what Rzehak and his colleagues "saw" over the course of the MTS Web Hosting project. What follows is his list of the good news and the bad.

Good news

» We have motivated people and we can shift business up to market level in a very fast way.
» We completed our project on time and within budget, and we helped our organization to understand a new business need.
» The project was a chance for every team member to jump into new themes, e.g. e-biz.

» We gained visibility as a finalist for the German project management award (from the Project Management Institute).
» We can offer the whole project as a solution.
» We gained a lot of know-how about the new economy, techniques, processes, and project management.

Bad news

» It's difficult to work in a virtual project organization, where it's hard for a project leader to address the people.
» It's difficult to change a big organization in a fast way. As a start-up project you have a lot of internal barriers.
» The entrepreneurship task in big organizations is at a very early stage.
» Our first target, going to market as a start-up with our own brand, didn't work out.

CHIYODA'S LNG PLANT FOR QATARGAS: AN AWARD-WINNING PROJECT

Building a liquefied natural gas (LNG) plant is an expensive, complex, dangerous task. Completing one of the largest plants constructed to date – ahead of schedule and within budget – in a remote, barren desert with a fragile ecosystem, no infrastructure, and virtually no available labor force is truly a remarkable feat. Accomplishing it earned Chiyoda Corporation the Project Management Institute's 1999 International Project of the Year award.[1]

Chiyoda Corporation of Yokohama, Japan won a contract to build two process units (known as "Trains") of a plant for Qatargas, a joint venture of the Qatar General Petroleum Co., Total SA, Mobil Corp., Mitsui & Co. Ltd, and the Marubeni Corp. Qatargas' mission was to build, own, and operate facilities to exploit and market LNG from the North Field gas reservoir in the Emirate of Qatar, thought to be the largest natural gas reserve in the world. As work on the first two Trains progressed, Chiyoda won another contract to build a third.

Valued at approximately US$2.3bn, the contracts' value and scale were among the biggest in Chiyoda's history. As important as the project was for Chiyoda, it was equally critical for the multinational consortium that contracted for it and for the host country. Because the project was a major milestone in the economy of Qatar, it had high visibility throughout, and was continually in the news as a showplace of Middle East economics.

Great expectations

At the start, the Chiyoda project managers announced their goal: "To complete the first and second LNG Trains two months early." They were being prudent, wanting to minimize the risk of unexpected delays and minimize costs. With the award of the contract for the third Train, their expectations grew even bolder, and they drew up a project schedule calling for completion of the third unit six months early.

Their optimism was well founded. Plant hand-over of the first Train occurred in September, 1996, 39 months from contract award, and the second Train was achieved three months later, both one month ahead of the contractual schedule. For the third Train, the project team outdid its own goal, handing it over in March 1998, 32 months from contract award and eight months ahead of schedule.

Against all odds

To achieve those results, the Chiyoda project team had to confront some formidable challenges, such as:

» *Complete absence of infrastructure.* Their site was nothing but desert, with summer temperatures approaching 120°F. The project's first task was to establish the necessary infrastructure. What was required was nothing less than a complete town for 9000 people about 75km from the Qatar capital of Doha. Along with housing and transportation services, the site required a power plant, desalination facilities for potable water, sanitation services including a wastewater disposal facility, and even recreation facilities. All this had to be accomplished with utmost attention to ecological and political issues, heightened by the need to work with a local community that was adjusting to the unfamiliar intrusion of a mega-project.

» *Lack of workforce*. There was virtually no available indigenous workforce. Most of the construction workers had to be brought in from outside the Emirate. In fact, Chiyoda mobilized workers from nearly 40 countries, resulting in project delays when work visas didn't come through promptly.

» *Acts of nature*. Even nature wasn't always on Chiyoda's side. Natural disasters in Japan and Europe slowed equipment deliveries and unusually heavy rains flooded the construction site, temporarily suspending work.

» *Currency fluctuations*. Revenue from Qatargas was in US dollars, but project expenses were in more than 10 currencies, so Chiyoda faced a real risk of foreign exchange fluctuations. For example, the exchange rate between the US dollar and the Japanese yen changed from ¥118.50/US$1 during the bidding stage to ¥88/US$1 by the middle of the project. To mitigate the risk of rate fluctuations, Chiyoda made foreign exchange rate contracts based on projected costs for each currency at an early stage of the project. These contracts fixed the rate between the dollar and the yen to avoid market fluctuations.

Chiyoda's approach to the project

Chiyoda began to confront the risks it could anticipate right from the time it decided to bid on the project. The company started engineering optimization studies during the bidding stage to permit a fast start if Chiyoda won the contract. It was a calculated risk but it paid off in two ways. First, it helped Chiyoda win the contract (one of the studies was a key factor in Chiyoda's winning bid) and, second, it gave the company a head start when project work began.

The project team

With a project this important and challenging, Chiyoda management took no risks in its choice of project team members. To fill key positions, it performed a special review of the entire company and selected only people with solid LNG project experience or those who were the best in their particular fields. The project manager – called the project director on this project – had worked for six LNG projects before this assignment and other key people had similar experience. So the project benefited from lessons they'd learned in the past.

To ensure timely decision-making, corporate management empowered the project director with a degree of authority equivalent to that of a corporate managing director. He got executive level support from the project sponsor, Chiyoda's executive vice president and general manager of the overseas project operation.

At the home office where the design, engineering and oversight occurred, the dedicated matrix-type project team numbered about 125, with about 200 more individuals from functional departments lending temporary support as needed. At the construction office, a site manager supervised construction and commissioning, supported by a staff of about 150 at its peak. All team members were encouraged to be creative and were rewarded on the basis of their individual participation and contribution to team goals.

Project management processes

Chiyoda spokespeople described their overall approach to project management processes as "planning, monitoring, and corrective action."

For managing the time and schedule, planning included scope and milestone schedule definition, detailed schedule development, and analysis. Monitoring required continuous schedule tracking, comparing actual progress with the detailed schedule, and forecasting the remaining duration through schedule analysis. Reports included the drawing schedule, procurement status report, three-month look-ahead report, and weekly construction schedule. When visa delays, equipment delivery slowdowns, and floods at the construction site wreaked havoc on the baseline project plan, the project team's detailed multitask scheduling permitted a rapid daily shift in work sequences.

For cost management, the plan consisted of a currency-wise detailed project execution budget and cash flow forecast. Monitoring involved collating cost data and computing a variance analysis, leading to whatever corrective action was necessary to maintain the budget. The project also had an effective cost change control system, which was used by Qatargas and Chiyoda as an overall control tool.

Quality management. Chiyoda acquired ISO 9001 certification a year after winning the project. To fully address Qatargas' quality requirements, Chiyoda developed a specific quality system for this project. It established a check-and-review system to ensure the implementation of engineering, procurement, and construction according to project requirements. It also instructed its subcontractors and vendors to establish their own quality assurance systems reflecting Chiyoda's requirements and consulted with them when necessary to ensure the highest standards were met.

The project document control team maintained on computer a master log of design drawings, specifications, subcontractors' submittals, and other documents to ensure that only the latest issues were used for design and construction. Chiyoda's inspectors and responsible engineers worked closely with subcontractors at the construction site and in vendors' factories, discussing the need for corrections as work proceeded. Chiyoda's site quality assurance team conducted daily and weekly quality surveillance reviews at the site.

Communications management. Projects flow on tides of communication, and this was no exception. Chiyoda operated a communication and data transmission system linking the project team and supporting divisions, Qatargas' home and overseas offices, the construction site office, and vendors. Being able to transmit data thousands of miles in real time resulted in considerable time, labor, and cost savings. Chiyoda transmitted all information via e-mail using Lotus Notes in combination with its internal Electronic Documents Management System, which was used to collect and compile technical information day by day in a secure and controlled manner.

Besides being able to transmit data, Chiyoda's headquarters was linked with the site in Qatar by an Intelsat digital communication system, which allowed videoconference, fax, and telephone.

Because the project had such visibility, it also required considerable external communications. While Qatargas handled most of this, the Chiyoda project team made audio/visual presentations and sophisticated computer-generated slideshows for presentation to various groups including dignitaries from Qatar, the United States, Europe, and Japan. It was essential for the project team to keep the government and people of Qatar in the forefront of all the activities during the construction and opening stages of the project. This project/host relationship culminated in a celebration to mark the plant opening hosted by His Highness the Emir, Shaikh Hamad Bin Khalifa Al-Thani.

Risk management. If there was one key to the project's success, it was probably this. At the outset, Chiyoda identified and developed responses for political risks, financial risks, risk associated with foreign exchange transactions, deficiencies in scope/specification or quality, and delay in delivery of material and equipment. In close cooperation with Qatargas, Chiyoda mitigated the effects of these by such risk management methods as forecasting the nature of risk, effective quantification, and effecting suitable countermeasures.

Results

Not only did the project come in ahead of time and within budget, it also achieved some important technical accomplishments including:

» removal of high levels of sulfur and mercaptan from field gas;
» enhanced sulfur recovery;
» satellite-linked electronic documents transmission; and
» development of various plant operation tools.

When the project came to an end, there was agreement among contractor, client, and host that it had met the essential criterion of building a reliable plant that would operate safely for 20–30 years.

LESSONS FROM QATAR

Chiyoda's project for Qatargas highlights several keys to success for an international project of this magnitude:

1 *Get a head start*. Chiyoda took a calculated risk and began engineering optimization studies during the bidding stage. Those studies gave Chiyoda a leg up on the competition in the bidding and got it off to a running start when work commenced.

2 *Aim higher than the specs require*. By aiming at completion dates even more ambitious than the project called for, Chiyoda had breathing room when delays occurred.

3 *Leave nothing to chance*. Chiyoda's careful risk management kept problems from becoming insurmountable.

4 *But expect the unexpected*. You can't anticipate everything. You're not going to prepare in advance for a flood in Europe that shut down an equipment factory (and yes, that happened to this project, too). But you can be ready to react quickly to any misadventure.

5 *Put your best people on the project* and reward them for individual innovation and for contributing to the team effort.

NOTE

1 This case study is adapted from an article by Masayuki Ishikura, Akira Kadoyama, and Yoshitsugi Kikkawa (January, 2000) "1999 International Project of the Year: Qatargas LNG plant project," in *PM Network*. This material is used with permission of the Project Management Institute Headquarters, Four Campus Boulevard, Newtown Square, PA 19073-2399, USA. Phone: (610) 356-4600, Fax: (610) 356-4647. Project Management Institute (PMI) is the world's leading project management association with over 70,000 members worldwide. For further information contact PMI Headquarters at (610) 356-4600 or visit the Website at www.pmi.org.

Key Concepts and Thinkers

» Words and phrases you need to know to talk the language
» The life cycle of a project
» Two keys to project success: change and risk management
» People you should know.

If you need a reference to check the meaning of unfamiliar terms, get a quick take on project management's core principles and processes, and meet some of its leaders, you're in the right place. Below is a glossary, followed by a discussion of key concepts, and an introduction to project management's pre-eminent thinkers.

GLOSSARY OF TERMS

Activity – A piece of work performed in carrying out a project. Often used synonymously with *task*, although the *PMBOK® Guide* defines a task as an even smaller subset of an activity.

Baseline – The original project plan, prior to making any changes.

Bottom-up estimating – A method of estimating the total cost of a project by first estimating the cost of each work item, then summing them into a total for the project. The smaller the work units, the more accurate the estimates will be.

Budget estimate – An assessment of the likely total cost of the project, usually including a range designated by plus/minus X%.

Change management – See Key concepts section below.

Charter – A document authorizing the implementation of the project. Most project charters contain, at a minimum, the project goals and scope, names of sponsor, project manager, and core team members, key stakeholders, and preliminary plan and cost estimate.

Contingency planning – Determining actions to be taken if identified risk events occur.

Contingency reserve – An amount of money or time set aside to accommodate events that cannot be planned for precisely in advance.

Cost budgeting – Determining each project component's share of the total cost estimate for the project.

Critical path – In a network diagram, the sequence of activities that determines the earliest possible completion date for the project. Technically, it is a path through the diagram that includes all the tasks that have no *float*.

Deliverables – Clearly defined outputs that must be produced at any stage of a project, including the final result.

Duration – The amount of time, expressed in work periods, such as workdays or workweeks, required to complete any activity or task.

Earned value analysis – A method of measuring project performance by comparing actual cost and schedule to what was planned.

Enterprise project management – Applying project management across the organization, running the organization as portfolios of projects. See also *Managing by projects*.

Float – In practical terms, this is the number of days you can delay starting a task without delaying the completion of the project. Tasks along the critical path don't have float. That's why the critical path determines the earliest possible completion date for the project.

Gantt Chart – A bar chart with activities listed down the left side and dates along the top. Date-placed horizontal bars show the sequence and beginning-to-end time of each activity.

Logical relationship – The precedence or dependency between tasks in a network diagram. A task that must be completed before another task is said to have precedence. A task that cannot be done until another is completed is said to be dependent.

Managing by projects – Using project management principles to structure and conduct work that has traditionally been treated as ongoing operations. See also *Enterprise project management*.

Matrix organization – An organizational structure in which much of the work is done by cross-functional project teams, led by project managers and staffed by experts drawn from functional units headed up by line managers. Upon completion of a project, team members revert to their functional units.

Network diagram – A schematic display of the project plan, drawn from left to right, illustrating the precedences and dependencies between tasks. Usually – but not always – tasks go into boxes connected by arrows.

PERT – Acronym for *Program Evaluation and Review Technique*, a method of estimating project duration using a formula that combines a weighted mix of three time estimates: most optimistic, most likely, and most pessimistic. The term *PERT Chart* is often incorrectly used for any network diagram.

Project – The work that needs to be done to produce a unique, predefined outcome within a predetermined time period and budget.

Project life cycle – See Key concepts section below.

Project management office – See *Project office*.

Project management – Applying appropriate skills, techniques, and tools so that a project is completed to specification, on time, and within budget.

Project office – A unit that coordinates projects across the organization, often providing standardized methods and tools and project management expertise. Sometimes called the *project management office*.

Project plan – A document that contains the project *scope* and *deliverables*, tasks to be done, *schedule*, assignments, communication plan, and budget, as well as assumptions, risk assessment, and contingency plans.

Project team – The people who direct and perform the work on the project. The core team is usually a small group of people who stay with the project for its duration, although they may continue to be responsible for regular jobs in line units of the organization.

Responsibility assignment matrix – A graphic representation of who is going to do what. Usually it lists tasks down one side and people along the top, designating responsibilities under each name. Also called *responsibility matrix*.

Risk management – See Key concepts section below.

Schedule – The sequence of tasks in a project with designated start and end dates for each, culminating in completion of the project. The schedule is often shown graphically on a *Gantt Chart*.

Scope – All the products and services to be included in the project. Often the scope definition includes not only what will be covered by the project, but also spells out which related projects and services will not be included.

Scope change – Any change in the project *scope*. Creeping scope change is often an issue in projects as project teams and stakeholders are tempted constantly to add "just this one thing," often affecting cost and schedule.

Sponsor – A high-level individual who provides authority for the project team to obtain resources and operate across the organization. Sponsors often assist in the preparation of documentation, advise on decisions that cross functional lines, and go to bat for the project team when obstacles arise.

Stakeholder – Anyone affected by the work or the outcome of a project. Can include customers, vendors, executives, managers of team members, and even people who may be adversely affected.

Task – A basic piece of work in a project, significant enough to be scheduled and tracked. See *activity*.

Top-down estimating – Estimating costs by guesstimates – educated guesses – usually at the executive level. This method is most often done at the early stages of project planning and replaced later by more accurate bottom-up estimating.

Work breakdown structure – A list or chart that includes all the tasks to be done in a project, organized into categories.

KEY CONCEPTS

Change management

Every plan changes as it is carried out. That doesn't mean a plan was wrong or that it is useless. The original plan is a baseline, a place to move out from. The impetus for change comes from many directions. Common stimuli include:

» personnel changes
» resource shortages
» budget cuts
» design failures
» advances by competitors
» requests to speed up delivery to meet customer requests or competitors' challenges
» management changes that can cause the project to lose or gain favor
» changes in organizational priorities
» new government regulations
» great new ideas that beg to be included.

Any of these can propel changes in how the project is carried out. Every project needs a change management process, an organized way to:

» identify necessary or value-added changes and avoid whimsical ones;
» keep senior management informed of worthwhile changes;

» get management approval to make changes that are outside the project manager's range of authority;

» document the changes made and update the plan.

Most change management processes follow steps like these:

1 Do a team assessment of the intended change. Determine its effect on scope, schedule, and budget. Identify any negative impacts. Involve everyone on the team who would be affected by the change.

2 Document the request for change. Include the reason for the change and the projected impact of the change on scope, schedule, and budget. Don't leave out any possible negative outcomes and risks involved.

3 Deliver the request for change to everyone who needs to review it. If it's a major change, be prepared to explain and defend it in face-to-face meetings.

4 When the change is approved, update the project plan (including the schedule and budget). Redo the network diagram, Gantt Chart, and any other project visuals. Post and circulate the new plan. Put the old plan away in the history file.

5 Circulate the revised plan to the group that approved the change.

6 Communicate the change to the entire team, clarifying how it changes their tasks and delivery dates.

7 Communicate the new plan to any stakeholders who did not have approval authority, clarifying the impact, if any, it has on them.

PROJECT LIFE CYCLE

Every project cycles through a series of phases, starting from an idea and ending when that idea becomes reality. Each phase has its own set of deliverables. Project phases vary somewhat from project to project, and the terminology for them differs from organization to organization. But there is a consistent pattern. One useful taxonomy, used by the pharmaceutical giant, GlaxoSmithKline, divides the life cycle into four phases: Conceptualization, Planning, Delivery, and Closure.

The major deliverables from each phase include:

Conceptualization – Project Charter, defining the purpose, intended outputs, scope of the project, and the core project team. The charter may also include a preliminary plan, along with the constraints and assumptions influencing that plan. The charter is used to obtain the commitment of all the stakeholders.

Planning – Baseline Project Plan, including project deliverables, tasks to be done, schedule, assignments, contingency plan, communication plan, and budget.

Delivery – Status reports, project review meetings, change requests, updates to project plan, schedule, and budget, and milestones achieved.

Closure – All deliverables to fulfill project goals, final financial accounting, full documentation of project, final reports to customers and management, and celebration.

In other books you may find the Conceptualization phase called Initiating and the Delivery stage broken into two, often called Executing and Controlling. But the term Conceptualization emphasizes that this is the thinking part, when you have to conceive, analyze, synthesize, and figure out just what this project needs to accomplish and how. And since executing and controlling occur simultaneously, the term Delivery effectively covers both.

RISK MANAGEMENT

Every project carries with it the risk of unexpected events that can delay it, cripple it, or even kill it. Risk management delivers those events out of the realm of unexpected and into the category of anticipated so the project team is prepared to handle them if they occur.

The first step is to identify potential risks, often done in a team brainstorming session. While every project has unique risks of its own, some risks hover over almost any project:

» Rising costs. Rising energy costs, wage increases, changes in vendors, higher costs of raw materials – any one of these could boost costs.
» Unavailable expertise. People with the right skills may not be available when needed. Crucial team members may leave.
» Inadequate time. If, for example, there are no available skilled people, training someone may destroy the project schedule.

» Undesirable effects. It's possible, for example, for a project to undermine other people's jobs. In that case the project may confront a powerful, resistant lobby.

» Changing technology or customer whims. There's an old story about the company that made the world's greatest buggy whip just in time for cars to arrive on the scene. These days almost every idea risks becoming a buggy whip before it gets off the ground.

» Political upheaval. In some companies, top management changes as fast as technology.

» Vendors may not provide exactly what you expect. Through misunderstandings, mismanagement of risks on their part, or even deceit, vendors don't always come through.

A brainstormed list of risks will contain some that are likely and some that are farfetched. The next step in managing risks is to identify those worthy of attention by estimating the probability of their occurring and the potential impact should they occur.

For those risks worth attending to, the *PMBOK® Guide* provides three categories of response:

» avoidance – eliminating the cause of the risk;
» mitigation – reducing the probability of the risk occurring or the cost if it does; and
» acceptance – acknowledging that the risk event may occur, and developing a contingency plan to deal with it when it does.

Some risks are avoidable. If a vendor has a track record of missed deadlines, it may be possible to switch to another. Other risks you can mitigate, with insurance perhaps or a service contract. But many risks fall into the acceptance category. Maybe the workload on one task will overwhelm the people assigned to it. A new system may have some bugs in it. Uncontrollable events may cause a cost overrun. For these risks, and others like them, contingency plans are crucial.

KEY THINKERS

David I. Cleland, PhD

In some circles David I. Cleland is known as the father of project management. It's an honor he's earned via nearly a half-century of practicing, teaching, and researching project management, more than 30 books he has authored or edited, and his scores of articles in periodicals and books.

The Project Management Institute elected him a fellow in 1987, twice awarded him the Distinguished Contribution to Project Management Award, and even named an annual award after him: the "David I. Cleland Excellence in Project Management Literature Award."

Professor Emeritus in the Department of Industrial Engineering at the University of Pittsburgh, Dr Cleland joined the department in 1967 after many years in the US Air Force as an instructor and a project manager in the development of weapon systems. He has also consulted in project management with companies in many different industries.

While he has lectured and written extensively on project management methodology, these days he's most interested in the organizational potential of project management as a strategic tool.

Project management, he asserts, provides a way to strategically manage the firm. He has a succinct definition of strategic management: "It's managing as if the future matters. I view projects as building blocks in the design and implementation of strategic management initiatives," he says.

Responding to environmental and competitive changes requires the development of new products, services, and organizational processes. "If you have a portfolio of projects dealing with these, reviewing it on a periodic basis is the best way for managers to get an understanding of how they are preparing the organization for the future."

As managers look at changes in the environment – economic, political, social, technological, and competitive – they begin to sense how those changes could impact their firm and develop strategies to take advantage of or protect against these changes. Carrying out each strategy requires a cross-functional effort within the firm, he explains, even bringing outside stakeholders into the effort. These efforts create continuing opportunities for project management in companies in all different industries.

"That's my interest now," Dr Cleland says. "To me the exciting part is making the linkage between project management and the organization's future."

Jon R. Katzenbach

Jon R. Katzenbach isn't a project management guru, but he has probably had more influence on the way people think about teams in business than anyone else. And projects require teams to do the work. So every project manager needs to know how teams function.

For many people, *The Wisdom of Teams*, the book Katzenbach co-authored with Douglas K. Smith, is the ultimate authority on the potential of teams and what's needed to achieve that potential.

When the book came out in the early 1990s, many people still shrugged off teams as a fad and asked, "Why bother?" The book's responses to that question are as powerful today as they were then.

» "First, [teams] bring together complementary skills and experiences that, by definition, exceed those of any individual on the team."
» "Second, in jointly developing clear goals and approaches, teams establish communications that support real-time problem solving and initiative."
» "Third, teams provide a unique social dimension that enhances the economic and administrative aspects of work ... people on teams build trust and confidence in each other's capabilities."
» "Finally, teams have more fun ... it both sustains and is sustained by team performance."[1]

Katzenbach's other books include *Real Change Leaders*, *Teams at the Top*, and *Peak Performance*. In addition, he is editor of *The Work of Teams*. He is a founder of Katzenbach Partners LLC and was formerly a director of McKinsey & Company, Inc.

Harold Kerzner, PhD

Harold Kerzner, professor of systems management at Baldwin-Wallace College in Berea, Ohio and executive director of the International Institute of Learning, is known as a master trainer. While he teaches project management skills to hundreds of students, managers, and candidates for Project Management Professional (PMP®) certification, he is equally riveted by the people side of leading project teams.

Historically, he says, project management was viewed as a scheduling tool to be used by engineers. But, he asserts:

"I have come to the belief that project management is more than planning and scheduling, but also working with teams, motivating them, getting them to complete an objective. The behavioral side is more important than quantitative techniques.

"If the behaviors are in place, you can take the worst possible plan and make it successful. But you can develop the greatest plan and if the people aren't motivated, they'll take you and your plan and bury you with it."

As focused as he is on both the quantitative and leadership skills of project managers, Dr Kerzner is equally absorbed in the organizational side of project management. "Companies realized that project management resulted in accomplishing more work in less time with fewer people," he says. "So they began to think, 'Maybe we can use it for smaller projects.'" That has led to three trends:

» Increased strategic planning for project management. Those companies with centralized project reporting systems, e.g. through an intranet, are using the information they acquire to assess how much business to take on and where to apply resources.
» Application of a single project management methodology across the company. The search for the best methodology to use contributes to the third trend.
» Benchmarking, not just to copy what companies are doing now, but also to project what project management will be like in the future.

Dr Kerzner asserts that:

"A lot of companies are realizing that project management is the survival of the firm. They want to sell their products and services to customers. They are saying, 'We provide solutions.' To sell a solution, they have to have project management skills to deliver."

Hans J. Thamhain, PhD

Hans Thamhain, professor of management at Bentley College in Waltham/Boston, Massachusetts, is a guru's guru. Author of several books and hundreds of articles on project management, he's been a major influence on other leading project management teachers and writers. Like many influential leaders in the field, he came from an engineering background, but he is as dedicated to the people side of project work as to the quantitative side.

One challenge for project leaders, he says, is that they have to earn their own authority. "The leader has only a small degree of authority given by the organization," he explains. "The rest you have to earn yourself. You earn it by demonstrating competence and by helping people do a good job. The team doesn't need a leader to do a good report, but rather to help resolve problems, get resources, resolve conflict, and create an environment that is professionally stimulating."

Another challenge is to build and hold together a team of part-timers. That's typical, he points out, especially in a matrix environment. The project manager, besides pulling the project together, has to have the leadership and persuasive skills to convince the functional resource managers that the project is important and to compete successfully for scarce resources.

The project team leader, he wrote in a recent article on "Leading without formal authority" for the *Project Management Journal*, is a "social architect who understands the interaction of organizational and behavioral variables and can foster a climate of active participation and minimal dysfunctional conflict."[2]

Dr Thamhain describes the need for project managers to have both quantitative and people skills. But he stresses that they aren't two separate, differentiated competencies. Rather, they are intricately linked.

"If anything," he says, "I shifted even stronger from managing by metrics to managing by people. But you cannot bring in a psychologist and think that will solve problems. You need the job skills and the administrative skills, and support systems. Without those, you lose credibility – and that brings us back to the human side."

NOTES

1 Katzenbach, J. R. & Smith, D.K. (1993) *The Wisdom of Teams*. HarperBusiness, New York.
2 Quoted from a pre-publication manuscript provided by the author.

Resources

» Books ranging from easy to in-depth
» Periodicals that keep up with the latest project management developments
» Two worldwide organizations for project managers and those who want to be
» What's hot on the Web for project managers.

Looking for more information about project management? There's a wealth of it out there. The hardest part is knowing where to start. To make that easier for you, here is a list of resources covering the range from basic to sophisticated, from conceptual to how-to's. It includes books, periodicals, organizations, and helpful Websites.

BOOKS

Amazon.com offered 1303 matches in response to a search for books on project management. That did not narrow the field very much, so here's a selection of classics, best sellers, and some personal favorites, organized into categories that should help you find what you need.

THE ONE AND ONLY...

A Guide to the Project Management Body of Knowledge (PMBOK® Guide), 2000 edn. Project Management Institute, Newton Square, Pa.

If there is a project management bible, this is it. The *PMBOK® Guide* describes the knowledge and practices "applicable to most projects most of the time," for which "there is widespread consensus about their value and usefulness." Most other literature and the majority of training programs are built on the nine project management knowledge areas described here: Project Integration Management, Project Scope Management, Project Time Management, Project Cost Management, Project Quality Management, Project Human Resources Management, Project Communications Management, Project Risk Management, and Project Procurement Management.

For anyone planning to pursue certification as a Project Management Professional (PMP®) by the Project Management Institute, this book is essential.

You can download sections of it free from PMI's Website, www. pmi.org.

COMPREHENSIVE REFERENCE BOOKS

» Cleland, D. I. & Ireland, L. R. (1999) *Project Manager's Portable Handbook*. McGraw-Hill, New York.

In a portable size, designed to be used as a job aid, this book gives advice on how to conceptualize, define, design, develop, and complete projects. But it's more than a how-to for managing an individual project. Written by two of the biggest names in the field of project management, it's also a guide to leading and motivating people and to organizing for managing projects across the enterprise.

» Forsberg, K., Mooz, H. & Cotterman, H. (2000) *Visualizing Project Management*. Wiley, New York.

A new edition of a highly popular how-to book. Generously illustrated with graphic models, this is a step-by-step guide to visualizing, then applying project management tools and techniques from the conception of a project to its completion. While acknowledging the value of sophisticated project management software, it also offers vivid low-tech techniques like the "cards-on-the-wall method" of identifying and arranging task dependencies with cards and string.

» Kerzner, H. (2000) *Project Management: A Systems Approach to Planning, Scheduling, and Controlling*, 7th edn. Wiley, New York.

Regularly updated, this is a standard for classroom and office. This book looks not only at the techniques of managing a project, but also at the larger context of the full job of the professional project manager. (One of its purposes is to help candidates prepare for PMI certification as a PMP®.) It talks about the location of project managers within both project-driven and non-project driven organizations, interfacing with line managers, working with executives, and project management as a springboard to higher level positions.

» Lewis, J. P. (1999) *The Project Manager's Desk Reference, A Comprehensive Guide to Project Planning, Scheduling, Evaluation, and Systems*, 2nd edn. McGraw-Hill, New York.

This is one of the best-selling project management reference books. The author offers the Lewis Method® of project management – an overall process – plus the "nitty-gritty procedures to be followed in carrying out the overall process." The book includes common causes of project success and failure and a section on "Other issues in project management," from communication skills to systems thinking, and including some specific applications such as managing business-to-business (B2B) projects.

» Pinto, J. K. (ed.) (1998) *The Project Management Institute Project Management Handbook*. Jossey-Bass, San Francisco, CA.

All the components of managing a project are here – but not from just one author's viewpoint. Instead, each topic is addressed by a different expert, with contributions from more than 25 leading academicians, consultants, and private industry practitioners. As well as how-to's, this book looks at human resources issues that project managers face and examines how project management fits into the larger context of business organizations.

INTRODUCTORY BOOKS

» *Baker, S. & K.* (2000) *The Complete Idiot's Guide to Project Management*, 2nd edn. Alpha Books, Indianapolis, IN.

Books in this popular series are not really for idiots. They are for people whose knowledge of the topic is limited or nonexistent, and who want to get up to speed fast. The breezy manner belies the authors' solid subject knowledge. This book is unintimidating but thorough.

» Deeprose, D. (2001) *Smart Things to Know About Managing Projects*. Capstone, Oxford.

Like other books in this series, this one provides an easy-to-read introduction to the fundamentals of the subject, along with insights from "gurus" and tips from practitioners. Experienced project managers contribute their best ideas and newcomers share lessons they've learned the hard way.

» Portny, S. E. (2000) *Project Management for Dummies*. Hungry Minds, Indianapolis.

Everything said above about the "Idiot's" book applies to this one as well. This is project management with a grin, but with substance too.

» Knutson, J. & Bitz, I. (1991) *Project Management: How to Plan and Manage Successful Projects*. AMACOM, New York.

This modest-sized book may not be the newest one in the bookstore, but it's clearly written, covers all the fundamentals, and is as applicable today as it was a decade ago.

THE ORGANIZATIONAL PERSPECTIVE

» Cleland, D. I. (1998) *Project Management: Strategic Design and Implementation*, 3rd edn. McGraw-Hill, New York.

This is a standard among project management guides, but it goes beyond process and techniques to focus on using projects to implement organizational strategies, especially for making changes in products, services, and processes. It also examines various team structures for carrying out projects in different kinds of organizations.

» Dinsmore, P. (1998) *Winning in Business With Enterprise Project Management*. AMACOM, New York.

How could anyone resist a book with chapter names like "Cookbooks, Restaurants, and Enterprise Project Management?" Written by a columnist for the magazine *PM Network*, this book's approach is anything but cookbook. It offers a guide to organizations that are serious about maximizing the benefits of project management by bringing oversight and consistency to the multitude of projects occurring independently throughout the enterprise.

» Graham, R. J. & Englund, R. L. (1997) *Creating an Environment for Successful Projects: The Quest to Manage Project Management*. Jossey-Bass, San Francisco.

This is a how-to book for upper management – advice for creating a project-based organization and developing project management as an organizational competency. The authors build their case for an organization-wide, integrated approach to project management on the experiences of such companies as Hewlett-Packard, AT&T, General Electric, and United Airlines.

» Kerzner, H. (2001) *Strategic Planning for Project Management Using a Project Management Maturity Model*. Wiley, New York.

The first part of this book makes the case that project management is a core competency, and companies had better start doing strategic planning for it. That starts with a gap analysis, comparing the company to its strongest competitor, then developing project management strategies to fill the gap. In the second part of the book, the author introduces a Project Management Maturity Model, which identifies five levels of development and counsels organizations on how to progress along the maturity curve.

THE PEOPLE SIDE

» Deeprose, D. (1998) *Recharge Your Team: Keep Them Going and Going*. . . . American Management Association, New York.

This is a very little book, just 74 pages, with advice from practicing team leaders on how to solve problems teams face as they mature. Includes symptoms, causes, actions, and preventative measures.

» Katzenbach, J. R. & Smith, D. K. (1993) *The Wisdom of Teams*. HarperBusiness, New York.

If you are going to buy just one book on teams, it should be this one – still the standard for the subject. The authors provide a thorough analysis of teams in business. Their definitions of team and high performance team are the ones most accepted by other authors, consultants, and businesses.

» Parker, G. M. (1995) *Cross-Functional Teams: Working with Allies, Enemies, and Other Strangers*. Jossey-Bass, San Francisco.

Focuses on creating a team approach that serves customers, based on experiences of 100 companies, including 3M, Motorola, and Honeywell.

» Robbins, H. & Finley, M. (2000) *The New Why Teams Don't Work*. Berrett-Koehler, San Francisco.

Despite the title, this book – an update of the author's popular *Why Teams Don't Work* – is more about why teams are worthwhile and how to make them work than it is about why they don't. It's got advice for team leaders, team members, and even for "teams of one."

AND A REALLY GOOD READ

» Kidder, T. (1981) *The Soul of a New Machine*. Little, Brown, Boston.

This isn't a book on project management *per se*, but it is one of the most engrossing stories of the life of a project – from conception to completion – you're likely to find anywhere. Kidder's book follows the development of a new computer back in the days when 32-bit minicomputers were the hottest thing. That computer may be out of date, but the struggle to create goes on.

PERIODICALS

International Journal of Project Management

This is the official journal of the International Project Management Association (IPMA). It is published bi-monthly by Elsevier Science, which has editorial offices in the United Kingdom, the United States, The Netherlands, Ireland, and Brazil. The journal covers all facets of project management, from systems to techniques to human aspects – with a strong international focus. The targeted audience includes researchers and lecturers in the academic world, as well as practitioners in business and industry. You can order a free sample issue from the Elsevier Website: www.elsevier.nl/inca/publications/store/3/0/4/3/5/index.*htt*.

PM Network

The professional magazine of the Project Management Institute (PMI), *PM Network* is published monthly by PMI. Its articles present details on how projects were managed and lessons learned from the project team experience. Regular features include software reviews, case studies, and organizational, legal, and other practical issues in managing projects. Columnist Chris Vandersluis usually takes a refreshingly irreverent approach to project management issues. In their column, Paula K. Martin and Karen Tate often discuss the people side of project management. Once a year, the magazine features PMI's Project of the Year. You can read sample articles on the PMI Website, www.pmi.org.

Project Management Journal

This is PMI's professional journal, published quarterly. The journal's editorial policy is to seek a balance among research, technique, theory, and practice. You can get more information on the journal from the PMI Website, www.pmi.org.

ORGANIZATIONS

If you've just read the descriptions above of project management periodicals, you already know there are two big organizations. Each has a claim to fame: the International Project Management Association

(IPMA) is the oldest and the Project Management Institute (PMI) is the biggest. Both have worldwide adherents.

International Project Management Association (IPMA)

Started in 1965 as a discussion group of managers of international projects, IPMA has developed into an international network of about 30 national project management societies with a total membership of 20,000. Headquartered in Switzerland, its activities include conferences, seminars, training programs, certification, newsletters and journals, and research. IPMA also sponsors activities for Young Project Managers, helping to educate students about project management and give them early experience. (For information on IPMA's Website, see below.)

Project Management Institute (PMI)

Headquartered in the United States, PMI has gone global via chapters in cities worldwide. Its total membership is over 75,000. PMI establishes project management standards and provides seminars and educational programs. It also conducts a certification program in project management, granting the Project Management Professional (PMP®) certification to those who meet its education and experience requirements and pass the certification examination. It publishes the project management bible, *A Guide to the Project Management Body of Knowledge (PMBOK® Guide)*. (You can learn more on the PMI Website; see below.)

USEFUL WEBSITES

Not only do the professional organizations offer information online, so do a myriad of consultants, from whose sites you can pick off some great ideas and job aids – many of them free. There are also discussion groups and reference sites. The list below is by no means exhaustive. It's part of a personal list of favorites that grows every time the words "project management" get entered into a search engine.

www.pmi.org

This is the place to go to find out about the Project Management Institute (PMI), the world's largest professional association for project managers. The site lists PMI's chapters and special interest groups, research programs, training and educational programs, and conferences and symposiums. There's information on its publications and you can read selections from the magazine, *PM Network*, online free. You can download, free, sections of the *Guide to the Project Management Body of Knowledge (PMBOK® Guide)*.

www.ipma.org

Look here for information about the International Project Management Association and its member associations and affiliated associations around the world. The site also announces conferences and training programs and describes the association's publications, programs for young project managers, and research into benchmarking. You can download the *IPMA Competence Baseline (ICB)* free, in three languages, English, French, and German. The *ICB* contains the elements of knowledge and experience in project management, personal attributes, and aspects of general impression that form the basis for national certification programs.

http://groups.yahoo.com/group/PM-Talk

This is a discussion group for sharing tips, tools, and techniques for managing projects. There are a lot of message strings focused on software. The group is particularly popular with newcomers looking for advice, but there seem to be plenty of old hands providing it.

www.fek.umu.se/irnop/projweb.html

This site is just what it calls itself: the WWW-Guide to Project Management Research Sites. It's a great place to start for doing Web research into project management.

www.iil.com

This is the Website of the International Institute of Learning, Inc., an organization specializing in project management training. Here you can download free a section of the company's program, "Project Management Basics™," including the segment, *Scheduling and Sequencing Tasks*. Nowhere will you find clearer instructions for calculating the critical path through a network diagram.

www.projectresults.com

One of the most practical and entertaining project management sites on the Internet, this is the home of MartinTate, consultants Paula Martin and Karen Tate, who are regular columnists for *PM Network* magazine. Click on Books/Products and you can download a generic project plan template and a preview of their *Memory Jogger* that by itself provides a clear map of the project management process. You can even read a medieval project management mystery novel or send a question to its heroine, who will provide down-to-earth answers expressed with twenty-first century sassiness.

www.michaelgreer.com

This site offers free handouts, with a propensity for lists, such as 10 Guaranteed Ways to Screw Up Any Project and 20 Key Project Manager Actions and Results.

http://cardboard.nu/checklists.html

This is the home of the Cardboard Scheduler, a project planning and tracking tool. The name still mystifies, but the site is generous about providing free useful checklists for every step of the project management process.

www.4pm.com

Website of the Hampton Group, 4pm.com has a discussion group where you can post questions to fellow project managers and join discussions of hot topics in project management.

Ten Steps to Making it Work

» Getting ready
» Gathering the team
» Creating a plan and budget
» Doing the work
» Celebrating success.

Are you getting ready to manage your first major project? Or are you up to your eyeballs in projects and feeling overwhelmed by the complexity of keeping them all on track? Either way, this chapter provides guidelines you can use to steer each project from great idea to completion.

This chapter isn't all you ever needed to know about managing a project, but it's a good start. Think of it as an itinerary for a journey. The resources in Chapter 9 provide additional guidebooks for getting the most out of every stop along the way.

CLARIFY THE PURPOSE

What business need will this project fulfill?

If this project was your idea, you will have to sell it to upper management. So you'll need to be real clear on what problem successful completion of this project will solve or what opportunity it will exploit.

On the other hand, you may have been assigned this project by upper management. In that case, you'll need to get clarity on the purpose or you may end up solving the wrong problem. Let's say you've been asked to manage the creation of a new Website. If you don't know that the value of the Website is going to be measured by how much product it sells, you might design one that wins awards for its esthetics – and fails miserably at fulfilling the real purpose of the project.

WRITE A PROJECT CHARTER

This is what you need for getting upper management's approval to proceed. But perhaps even more important is that in writing a project charter, you do the necessary upfront analysis and initial organizing that sets you off on the right track. So gather a small, dedicated team (two or three at this stage) and go to work. If your company has a project office, that office probably has a charter template. If not, be sure to include these things:

» *The business purpose the project will address,* including:
  » problem or opportunity
  » strategic initiative it supports
  » business risks of not doing this project.
» *The project sponsor.* Every project needs one, ideally someone one or more levels up the organization from you, who is as dedicated

as you are, can provide authority for your project team to obtain resources and operate across the organization, and will go to bat for the project when obstacles arise.

» *Your project outputs or deliverables*. When the project is finished, what will you have that you didn't have before? Make these clear and specific.

» *The project scope*. What the project will and won't encompass, including:

  » product specifications – quality, quantity, performance, reliability, even governmental standards if they apply. To the extent you can, make each attribute measurable;

  » project objectives – not only output, but timeframe and estimated costs. Make it clear the estimates are guesses only, based on your own and others' past experience but subject to change; and

  » project constraints. Talk to everyone who can help you recognize if there are resource (people, equipment, financial), time, organizational, legal, or other restrictions that will limit what you can do.

» *Assumptions you are operating under*, concerning such issues as:

  » available skills and expertise

  » money you expect to get for the project

  » what that money will buy, in terms of outside and inside resources

  » related business needs that will be filled in some other way.

» *A plan overview* – including major milestones and interim deliverables on your way to your final outcome and a schedule for attaining them.

» *Your team*. The few who are already working with you and your recommendations for a group that can oversee all the work that needs to be done.

» *How you are going to communicate with upper management, your sponsor, stakeholders, and team members* – what reports, meetings, briefings, etc. will keep everyone apprised of your progress.

BUILD A DYNAMITE PROJECT TEAM

Leading and motivating the people who work on the project will be one of your main responsibilities throughout all the subsequent steps to completing a successful project.

The key thing that distinguishes managing a project team from managing a line operation is that, in all probability, the people who do the work won't report to you. Yes, some organizational authority lent them to the project for a certain period of time, but many of them will still be expected to keep up with their ongoing work in their regular jobs. So their loyalties will be divided at best and, when push comes to shove, it will be the project that gets shoved aside – unless they feel the same passion for it that you do. You can't win them over by authority, but you can do it through influence, and that's pretty powerful.

You have to earn influence. You can do that through demonstrating the following.

» *Expertise*. People will look to you for leadership when you know more than they do about a key subject. You won't be an expert in every team task, but you can and must understand the big picture better than anyone else on the team. And you must be willing to share that understanding with everyone.
» *Relationship building*. Get out of your office and get to know people personally. If you can, start the relationship building before you ever need a person's help on a project. Spread a few favors around; people remember and will be there when you need them.
» *Respect for others*. Listening well is key here, especially listening without passing judgment. Accepting others' decisions shows respect too. So does welcoming feedback from others on your behavior.
» *Trustworthiness*. People are comfortable allowing themselves to be influenced by someone they trust to tell the truth (both good and bad), give credit where it is due, accept accountability when things go wrong, and care more about the outcome of the project than about personal aggrandizement.

To become an effective team leader, a good place to start is with six guidelines offered by Jon R. Katzenbach and Douglas K. Smith, in their book, *The Wisdom of Teams*.[1]

» Keep the purpose, goals, and approach relevant and meaningful.
» Build commitment and confidence.
» Strengthen the mix and level of skills.

» Manage relationships with outsiders, including removing obstacles.
» Create opportunities for others.
» Do real work.

PLAN AND SCHEDULE THE WORK

If you thought you did that in Step 2, think again. That was the tip of the iceberg to get the project off the ground. Now is when the real work starts. Get your team together (this is neither a one-person nor a one-session job) and:

» *Create a work breakdown structure (WBS)*. A WBS contains all the tasks that have to be done to complete the project, organized into categories. You can create one in either outline or chart form, usually displayed in levels with major deliverables at the higher levels and detailed tasks at the lowest levels.

For a large project, you would probably break your WBS into sequential stages. You could organize a project for building a new office, for example, into stages such as design, contracting, building, decorating, landscaping, and moving in. At the outset you'd only need to determine the individual tasks for the design stage. You could fill in the detailed tasks for the other stages as the time approached to begin work on them.

» *Sequence the tasks*. The tool for doing this is the network diagram, which is really a map of the project. The network diagram uses boxes connected by arrows to sequence all the tasks from left to right chronologically, showing at a glance which tasks have to be done before another one can be started (precedences), which can be done concurrently, and which are totally independent of each other. In simplified form, a typical network diagram looks something like Fig. 10.1, with the boxes representing tasks.

» *Calculate how long the tasks will take*. Start by estimating the duration of each task. PERT (Program Evaluation and Review Technique) provides a sophisticated method for doing this using a formula that combines a weighted mix of three time estimates: most optimistic, most likely, and most pessimistic. For many projects, you won't need to use PERT; you'll probably use your best judgment (based

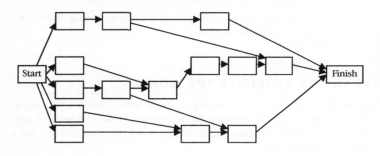

Fig. 10.1

on good research). But don't forget to make allowances for "most pessimistic." It can happen.

You don't need to add the durations of all the tasks to calculate the total time because you'll be doing some of them concurrently. But you do need to add up those on the "critical path." There is a formal method of calculating the critical path, which you will need to learn for major projects, but for smaller ones, you can do it this way: Write the time estimate (duration) for each task into the boxes in the network diagram. Now think of the lines on the diagram as roads, and you'll see that there appear to be various roads that go from start to finish. Add up the durations of the tasks along each of these alternate roads. The longest one is the critical path – and the shortest time in which you can complete the project.

To illustrate, Fig. 10.2 shows the network diagram from above, with hypothetical durations in days for each task. If you add the durations for the different "roads" you'll see the one in bold is the longest, hence it is the critical path.

» *Create a schedule*, by translating the durations of all the tasks into calendar dates and accommodating any unanticipated problems, such as holidays that fall in the middle of a critical task or resources not available at a particular time. The most popular way to display a schedule is on a Gantt Chart, a bar chart with activities listed down the left side and dates along the top. Date-placed horizontal bars show the planned sequence and beginning-to-end time of each

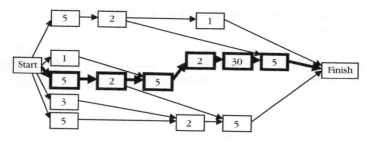

Fig. 10.2

activity. (Project management software will create Gantt Charts that also show precedences among tasks.) Later you'll add bars with actual times to produce a vivid illustration of how well you are meeting your schedule.

» *Assign people to the tasks*. You'll need to balance who has the best skills for each task, who wants to do it, who is available, and who works well with the other people assigned to the same or interdependent tasks. Unless your project is mega-sized, many of the people on your project team will probably be working on the project part-time, balancing it with a full-time ongoing job and perhaps another project or two. So you'll need to negotiate for their time with them and their line managers. The project sponsor can often help a lot here.

To keep track of who is doing what, the tool of choice is the responsibility assignment matrix, a table with people listed across the top and tasks down the side.

Project management software, such as Microsoft Project™, is a great planning and scheduling tool. It will provide templates to fill in all your project information, draw your charts and tables for you, even update all the pieces when you make a change in any one. But it won't do your thinking, identify the tasks to be done, figure out how long it will take to do them, or choose the right people.

ANALYZE RISKS AND PREPARE CONTINGENCY PLANS

Murphy's Law will strike, count on it. So prepare in advance. Get the team together and brainstorm all the "what ifs" you can come up with. Here are some typical ones to get you started:

» costs go up
» expertise is unavailable
» tasks take longer than expected
» you hit unexpected resistance somewhere else in the organization
» technology or customer needs change
» your company reorganizes
» vendors fail to deliver.

You are bound to come up with others specific to your project.

When you have a complete list, rate the probability and the potential impact of each item. Your ratings will tell you which you need to deal with right now, and which you really should prepare for . . . just in case. Once you've identified them, you may be able to eliminate some risks or at least reduce the chance they will occur. You might, for example, choose a different vendor if your favorite one has been missing deadlines lately.

But other risks you'll just have to accept, and develop a contingency plan so you are ready if they occur. Let's say, for example, the vendor who misses deadlines is the only one producing the item you need. In that case, you'd better have a Plan B to switch to so you can accommodate later delivery from the vendor.

DEVELOP A BUDGET

This step and the previous one are not perfectly sequential. You won't wait until after you have created your complete plan and schedule and assigned people to each task before asking, "Oh yeah, how much is this all going to cost?" There will always be tradeoffs among your schedule, your resources, and your finances, so all of them have to be worked on in tandem.

To develop a budget, you estimate your expenses and then allocate the total among your tasks, or deliverables, over time. Easier said than done, of course.

To start, the estimates you included in your charter need to be refined now. You or upper management probably arrived at those numbers by educated guesses. They could easily be off by plus/minus 25%, maybe even by up to 100%.

You can improve them by bottom-up estimating, a process based on the assumption that the total is the sum of the parts. To do this, you estimate the cost of each work item, then sum them all up into a total for the project. To do your estimates, be sure to consider:

» all the work to be done;
» all the resources – equipment, space, labor;
» unit rates for each resource – e.g. weekly rates for rented equipment;
» time – e.g. how long you will need that rented equipment;
» experience – lessons from similar projects in the past; and
» your contingency plans. Don't forget to provide for them.

Multiply each resource unit rate by the time needed and sum up the outcomes. Then temper that by past experiences, your contingency plans, and your good judgment. Now you've got an estimate you'll do your best to live by.

But a budget is more than a cost estimate. It's also a tool to track your performance progress. So you will need to allocate your cost estimates by task and by reporting period, perhaps monthly. That requires another close examination of your resource assignments to determine what your needs will be at any point in time. For a fairly simple project, you now transfer that information onto a spreadsheet with expense categories down the side and reporting periods along the top, with space to fill in estimates now and actual spending as the work progresses. For a bigger project, you'll need such forms for each milestone, or even each task. At that stage, project management software helps a lot.

EXECUTE THE PLAN

When the time comes to put the plan into action, it is the project manager's job to stay on top of all the action to ensure continued progress toward the project goal and to keep upper management informed. Most project managers do that through a combination of face-to-face meetings and written reports, although company intranets are increasingly replacing paper as the standard medium for the latter.

Project tracking processes usually include:

» *Task status reports from the team members*, covering tasks completed, current tasks with projected completion dates, outcomes, expenditures, issues and recommendations, next steps, questions, and approvals needed. You may want these weekly or monthly, the latter supplemented by more frequent exception reports.

» *Project status reports from the project manager to team members*, usually built around scope, time, and cost, comparing actual to planned with corrective actions where necessary.

» *Status reports for sponsor, management, and other stakeholders*, including customers or others whose work your project impacts. The sponsor will probably want details, but others might prefer exception reports only, focusing on red issues and planned corrective actions. Your sponsor and management may prefer to get these reports in person at regularly scheduled meetings.

» *Regular meetings with the team*, to cover deadlines, actions, issues and accountabilities; to meet with subject experts when necessary; and for team problem solving and decision making.

» *Informal meetings with team members*. Project managers usually learn more by being accessible than by reading reports. When you lead a project team, don't neglect drop-in visits and casual phone calls.

MANAGE CHANGES

Don't ever doubt it; there will be changes in scope, cost, and/or time. You may have to contend with personnel changes, resource shortages, budget cuts, design failures, requests that you speed up delivery, changes in organizational priorities, government regulations. Mistakes happen, and you have to compensate. Or, at the other extreme, you or someone else may have a great new idea that you just have to incorporate. You may have contingency plans in place for some situations, but others may blindside you.

To cope, you'll need a change management system – an organized way to differentiate between changes that add value and those that don't, inform senior management of worthwhile changes, get approval to make changes, document them, and update the plan. For more on change management see Key concepts and thinkers in Chapter 8.

BUILD AND MAINTAIN RELATIONSHIPS OUTSIDE THE TEAM

Just because this is Step 9 in the list doesn't mean you can wait until the project is almost over to do it. It's another of the steps that has to be done in concert with the rest of your project management work.

As a project manager, it's your job to:

» *Keep upper management and your customers up-to-date.* Don't let your project suffer while you wait for a scheduled meeting to resolve an issue. Arrange for a liaison you can go to when you can't reach the highest-ranking person reviewing your project.

» *Maintain links with other teams working with projects related to yours.* You may be able to cooperate with another team in some aspects, to the benefit of both. At the very least you can avoid competing for resources, stepping on toes, or reinventing each other's wheels.

» *Build relationships with your end users.* Get a confirmed handle on the users' wants and needs, develop their trust in you, and build up anticipation for your product or service.

» *Find a common language with all your stakeholders.* If you are working with people in a function you are unfamiliar with, don't assume your understanding and theirs is the same. Find an interpreter fluent in both functions to help you spell out your agreements in ways neither of you misinterpret.

COMPLETE THE PROJECT AND CELEBRATE

Finally, a step that really is in sequence.

When the final output defined in your project charter and project plan is complete, it's time to close down the project. But before you move on, you'll need to do the following:

» *Verify that all promised deliverables are complete.* Make sure nothing has fallen through the cracks.

» *Create a list of loose ends that need to be tied off.* With the team, prioritize, schedule, assign, and do the actions needed.

» *Confirm with the customers, upper management, and other stakeholders that all project outputs have been accomplished* to their satisfaction.

» *Notify team members in writing when the project will end.* This shouldn't come as a surprise to them. The written notification is for their records.

» *Notify their managers in writing when the project will end* and team members will be free to work full-time back at their work units.

» *Notify all vendors in writing when their services will no longer be required.* Again, this should be a formality, not a surprise.

» *Release any leased or borrowed equipment.*

» *Close the books on the project.* Complete the final financial accounting.

» *Hand off responsibility to permanent staff* if your project turns into an ongoing program to be run by others.

» *Celebrate.* This isn't a fun option. It's as important as your final report. Ending on a high note prepares people to move on with energy.

» *Write thank-you letters to everyone who touched the project* – team members, their bosses, advisors, people whose advice you sought, managers who lent you equipment or office space, vendors, and, of course, customers.

» *Complete your documentation of the entire project* – the steps you took, the changes you made, the problems you encountered, the actions taken to solve them, the shortcuts and better methods the team discovered, the issues with vendors, what worked better than you expected, and what you'd do differently next time. All these things go into your historical record for the benefit of anyone who takes on a similar project in the future.

» *Prepare your final reports for customers and management.* At the very least these should include major accomplishments; a comparison of end results to original goals, specifications, and projected schedule; final financial accounting; a description of how the project was organized; achievements of individual team members; and recommendations for follow-up.

» Congratulate yourself, take a deep breath, and move on to your next project.

NOTE

1 Katzenbach, J. R. & Smith, D. K. (1993) *The Wisdom of Teams*. HarperBusiness, New York.

Frequently Asked Questions (FAQs)

Q1: Why do I need project management skills when I work in a company that is organized functionally?

A: See Chapter 1, paragraph that begins "But all that work..."

Q2: How does managing a project differ from managing ongoing work?

A: See Chapter 2, under "Project management: what makes it different?"

Q3: Where did project management tools and methodologies come from?

A: See Chapter 3.

Q4: What is a virtual project team?

A: See Chapter 4 under "The rise of the virtual project team."

Q5: What difficulties should I expect to face working on a project in another country?

A: See Chapter 5 under "Culture shock."

Q6: Should my company set up a dedicated project office?

A: See Chapter 6 under "Centralized support and oversight" and "The skeptics."

Q7: What can a project manager do when the company changes the rules midstream?

A: See Chapter 7 under "Siemens' MTS Web Hosting Project" and Chapter 8 under "Change management."

Q8: How can I prepare for all the unexpected things that might occur and disrupt my project?

A: See Chapter 8 under "Risk management."

Q9: What organizations can I join to learn more about project management and network with people who are doing it?

A: See Chapter 9 under "Organizations."

Q10: Help, I've been assigned to manage my first project. What do I do?

A: See Chapter 10.

Index

activity   78
added value analysis   7
Apollo Space Project   15, 19
audits   48
automated Web hosting   63–9
Automotive Systems Group (ASG)
   51

Baker, S. K.   92
baseline   78, 81, 83
benchmarking   46, 47–8, 87
Bickel, Mike   31–2, 45–6
Bitz, I.   92
bottom-up estimating   78, 107

Cardboard Scheduler   98
case studies   58–75
change management   81–2, 108–9
charter   78, 82–3, 100–101
Chiyoda Corporation   69–75
Cleland, David I.   43–5, 53–4, 84–5,
   85, 90–91, 93
closure   83
collectivism   37
common language   46, 109
communication, case study
   66–7, 73

completion   109–11
concepts   81–4
contingency planning   78
contingency reserve   78
continuous improvement   46, 47
cost budgeting   78, 106–7
cost change control system   72
cost management   72
Cotterman, H.   91
CPM *see* Critical Path Method
critical path   7, 78, 98, 104, 105
Critical Path Method (CPM)   14, 19
Cultural Value Dimensions   36–8
culture clash   35–40
customers   10, 24, 26–7, 28, 109,
   110–111

decision-making   65, 72
Deeprose, D.   92, 94
deliverables   78, 101
delivery   83
Dinsmore, Paul   49–50, 52, 93
dot.coms   22
Du Pont   14, 19
duration   78

e-business projects   25–7
e-communications   21–8

earned value analysis   79
Electronic Documents Management System   73
Englund, R. L.   93
enterprise project management   15, 49-53, 79
    see also managing by projects
environment   85
extranets   24

femininity   37-8
Finley, M.   94
Fleisher, Michael   60-61
float   79
Forsberg, K.   91
frequently asked questions   113-14

Gantt Chart   7, 12-13, 18, 79, 104-5
Gantt, Henry   12-13, 18
Garner Alumni Connect   58-63
global project management   29-40
glossary   78-81
Graham, R. J.   93
Groves, General Leslie R.   13
A Guide to the Project Management Body of Knowledge (PMBOK™)   7, 17, 46, 49, 84, 90, 97

history   11-20
Hofstede, Geert   36-8
Hoover Dam   13

individualism   37
Institute of Civil Engineers of Great Britain   14
inter-team liaison   60, 109
International Institute of Learning, Inc.   97-8
International Journal of Project Management   95
International Project Management Association (IPMA)   15-16, 19, 95-6, 97

INTERNET   15, 19, 24, 26-7
intranets   23-4, 28, 67
IPMA *see* International Project Management Association
IPMA Competence Baseline (ICB)   97
Ireland, L. R.   90-91

Katzenbach, John R.   9, 86, 94
Kerzner, Harold   9, 35-6, 45-6, 86-7, 91, 93, 102-3
key aspects
    concepts   81-4
    frequently asked questions   113-14
    ten steps   99-111
    thinkers   84-8
Kidder, Tracy   24, 94
Knutson, J.   92

LAN *see* Local Area Network
leadership   8-9, 54-5, 65, 88, 102
Lewis, J. P.   91-2
line managers   43, 47
liquefied natural gas (LNG) plant   69-75
Local Area Network (LAN)   23
logical relationship   79
long-term orientation   38
Lotus Notes™   3, 73

managing by projects   2-4, 15, 79
    see also enterprise project management
Manhattan Project   13, 19
Marshall, Bill   31
masculinity   37-8
matrix organization   15, 17-18, 19, 43, 79, 88
mentoring   47
methodology   47, 52, 87

Mooz, H. 91
MTS Web Hosting project 63-9

National Aeronautics and Space
Administration (NASA) 15
network diagram 79, 103, 104, 105
networks 22-3, 25
Newell, Michael W. 49
Nortel Networks 30-35, 45-6

operations management 7-9
Oppenheimer, J. Robert 13
optimization studies 71, 74
Oracle database 32
organizations 42-55
books 93
global project management
29-40
matrix organization 43
strategy 44-6
see also enterprise project
management; managing by
projects

Parker, G. M. 94
periodicals 95
PERT (Program Evaluation and
Review Technique) 7, 14, 15, 19,
79, 103
Peters, Tom 3
Pinto, J. K. 92
planning 8, 71, 72, 80, 82-3,
100-101, 103-5
PLUS (Product Launch System) 51
PM Network 95, 97
*PMBOK*TM *Guide see Guide to the
Project Management Body of
Knowledge*
PMI *see* Project Management Institute
PMPTM *see* Project Management
Professionals
Polaris 14, 19

Portny, S. E. 92
power distance 37
project, definition 6-7, 79
project life cycle 82-3
*The Project Management Body of
Knowledge* 17, 19
Project Management Institute (PMI)
90, 92, 96
Cleland 85
enterprise project management
50
history 16-17, 19
International Project of the Year
award 69
periodicals 95
theory of project management 54
Website 97
*see also A Guide to the Project
Management Body of
Knowledge*
Project Management Journal 95
project management maturity 46
project management processes
46-8, 72-4
Project Management Professionals
(PMPTM) 16-17, 19
project managers
case study 72
change management 82
leadership 8-9, 54-5, 65, 88, 102
matrix organization 43
project offices 48-9
project office 46-9, 80
project plan 64, 80, 82

quality management 73-4

Rand Remington Univac 14, 19
reporting, matrix organization 43
responsibility, teams 9-10
responsibility assignment matrix 7,
80, 105

risk management   74, 83–4, 106
Robbins, H.   94
Rzehak, Wolfgang   64–6, 68–9

SBS *see* Siemens Busines Services
schedule   13, 72, 80, 103–5
scientific management   12
scope   80, 101
scope change   26–7, 80
SDT *see* Simultaneous Development
  Teams
short-term orientation   38
Siemens Busines Services GmbH & Co
  OHS (SBS), case study   63–9
Simultaneous Development Teams
  (SDT)   51
singular methodology   46
Smith, Douglas K.   9, 86, 94, 102–3
software
  books   91
  enterprise project management
    52
  history   18, 19
  LANs   23
  projects   26
  scheduling   105
  Websites   98
sponsor   80, 100
stakeholders   24, 81, 82, 109, 110
standardization   30–40, 46–8, 51
strategic management   44–6, 85
success, definition   10
supply chain management   31, 32,
  34

task, definition   81
Taylor, Frederick   12
teams   88, 101–3
  books   94
  case study   71–2

change management   82
communication   66–7
critical characteristics   9–10
definition   9, 80
development   65–6
e-messages   22–3
inter-team liaison   60, 109
Katzenbach   86
leadership   8–9, 54–5, 65, 88, 102
multinational   35–40
project office   48
responsibility   9–10
virtual project team   25, 28, 64, 69
Thamhain, Hans J.   53, 54–5, 87–8
theory of project management   53–4
thinkers   84–8
time   6–7, 38, 72
tools   7–8, 22–3, 32–3, 42
  see also software
top-down estimating   81
training   33–4, 46, 47

uncertainty avoidance   38

vendors   62, 73, 84
virtual project team   25, 28, 64, 69
Viscardi, Julie   58–63
Volpe, Kevin   61–2

WAN *see* Wide Area Networks
Warren, Kathleen   58–62
WBS *see* work breakdown structure
Web projects   22
Websites   23–4, 26–8, 33, 58–63, 67,
  96–8
Wide Area Networks (WANs)   23
work breakdown structure (WBS)
  81, 103

"Yucee"   66–9

Printed and bound in the UK by
CPI Antony Rowe, Eastbourne

Printed and bound by CPI Group (UK) Ltd, Croydon, CR0 4YY

13/04/2025

14656564-0001